D1403670

of the mediocre and the ordinary to the rarified air of an extraordinary life. What an adventure!"

—DR. JAY STRACK, president and founder, Student Leadership

"For as long as I have known Doug, this book's message has been the passion of his life: to live every day with a constant awareness of the presence of God and to help others do the same. *More Than Ordinary* provides practical wisdom on the often vague concept of walking with God. The book is deeply personal, real, transparent, and inspirational. It is a game-changing read!"

—MARK BANKORD, founder and directional leader,
Heartland Community Church, Rockford, Illinois

"As you read *More Than Ordinary*, you will discover a man who has had an astounding walk with our Lord and a passion for sharing it with others. Doug is a wonderful motivator who challenges me to a deeper, daily, hourly walk with my Lord, and I believe that you will feel the same as you read this book."

—CLYDE JACKSON, CEO, Wynne/Jackson, Dallas, Texas

"Doug Sherman's book *More Than Ordinary* created in me a new depth of understanding and experience in practicing the presence of God. I shall never be the same."

—JOHN BISAGNO, pastor emeritus, Houston's First Baptist Church

"Don't give up! You really can have the deep, satisfying, personal relationship with God that you've always wanted. For many of us, that 'best Friend' relationship seems elusive—a nice idea, but not very workable in real life. But Doug Sherman shows us how. By his own example, he lets us see how we, too, can have a more-than-ordinary, daily adventure with God as we choose to do life with Him."

—CYNTHIA HYLE BEZEK, editor of *Pray!* magazine (www.praymag.com);
author of *Come Away with Me* and *Prayer Begins with Relationship*

"Too many of us have faulty conceptions of God that keep us from experiencing His personal presence in our daily lives. In *More Than Ordinary*, Doug Sherman helps us tear down walls of misunderstanding and build a foundation for an extraordinary relationship with our Creator. This is an honest, practical, and encouraging book for all who have a desire to go deeper with Christ. It will nourish your soul!"

—T. J. ADDINGTON, senior vice president,
Evangelical Free Church of America; leader, ReachGlobal

MORE THAN ORDINARY

ENJOYING LIFE WITH GOD

DOUG SHERMAN

= WITH TERRA MCDANIEL =

NAVPRESS

Discipleship Inside Out™

NavPress is the publishing ministry of The Navigators, an international Christian organization and leader in personal spiritual development. NavPress is committed to helping people grow spiritually and enjoy lives of meaning and hope through personal and group resources that are biblically rooted, culturally relevant, and highly practical.

For a free catalog go to www.NavPress.com
or call 1.800.366.7788 in the United States or 1.800.839.4769 in Canada.

ISBN-13: 978-1-61521-616-1

Cover design by Brady Clark

Some of the anecdotal illustrations in this book are true to life and are included with the permission of the persons involved. All other illustrations are composites of real situations, and any resemblance to people living or dead is coincidental.

Unless otherwise identified, all Scripture quotations in this publication are taken from the New American Standard Bible® (NASB), Copyright © 1960, 1962, 1963, 1968, 1971, 1972, 1973, 1975, 1977, 1995 by The Lockman Foundation. Used by permission. Other versions used include: the *Holy Bible, New International Version*® (NIV®). Copyright © 1973, 1978, 1984 by International Bible Society. Used by permission of Zondervan. All rights reserved; and *THE MESSAGE* (MSG). Copyright © 1993, 1994, 1995, 1996, 2000, 2001, 2002. Used by permission of NavPress Publishing Group.

Library of Congress Cataloging-in-Publication Data
Sherman, Doug.
  More than ordinary : enjoying life with God / Doug Sherman with Terra
McDaniel.
     p. cm.
  Includes bibliographical references (p.   ).
  ISBN 978-1-61521-616-1
  1. Spiritual life--Christianity. I. McDaniel, Terra. II. Title.
  BV4501.3.S536 2011
  248.4--dc22
                                         2011013600

Printed in the United States of America

1 2 3 4 5 6 7 8 / 16 15 14 13 12 11

To my amazing children, Jason, Matt, and Jennie; their spouses, Katie, Kayla, and Justin; and our grandchildren—and to both their generations—with hopes that you will go much further than I have in enjoying God so you will experience Him in richer and more exciting ways than you ever imagined!

CONTENTS

FOREWORD

Stale. Legalistic. Emotional. Disciplined. Determined. Frustrated.

Do any of these words describe your spiritual pilgrimage? If they do, you will be refreshed by Doug Sherman's *More Than Ordinary*. It is a personal, intense, and transparent door to his personal struggles and subsequent discovery of how to practically encounter and enjoy God. From the emotional reality of his teen years to his attempts to please God and work for God, you will enter a journey of rediscovery and freedom. This is powerful and real! It will open the door to a renewed relationship with Jesus. This book brings the truth of Scripture to a realistic walk with Christ. There are no gimmicks or shortcuts, just a steady and compelling guide to a new level of spiritual encouragement and freedom. *More Than Ordinary* will lead you down an astonishing path of discovery in your spiritual journey.

Almost everyone struggles with living an authentic life as a follower of Jesus. We try hard. We stumble around. We read the Bible and books focused on the felt needs of our lives. We experience moderate success but still long for something "more, deeper, intense, real"—or words to that effect. Disciplines have become dry. Profound biblical effect on our inner selves and our outward lives of work, marriage, and family seems elusive at best and fraudulent at worst. I can attest to those struggles in my own life.

More Than Ordinary strikes at the root of these dilemmas.

I have known Doug since his days as a cadet at the U.S. Air Force Academy and had the privilege of being a small part of his growth as a follower of Christ. He was young, self-assured, and clearly a leader. I was a young officer on the faculty and had observed hundreds of young men. I knew that Doug would do well in the Air Force or in whatever he set his mind on doing. Doug was an energetic leader and an influencer in our fledgling Navigator ministry at the "Zoo," our nickname for the Air Force Academy. It was a hothouse for emerging leaders. It was also a fertile ground for the gospel and for spiritual growth.

When I read the draft of *More Than Ordinary,* I was deeply moved and encouraged. I almost immediately called Doug and said, "Doug, I didn't know so many of the details of your early life. Why didn't you share them with me when we were meeting?" His reply was both sobering and insightful. "Jerry, I was deeply ashamed. I didn't want anyone to know." I now wonder how many who read this will recall their own untold stories.

This book is not an exclamation mark or a mathematical "q.e.d." (e.g., problem solved) placed at the end of a proof. It is a journey. It is a powerful description of an ongoing process. It is more than just a description of the spiritual walk and decisions personal only to Doug Sherman. It lays out a path to a deeper discovery of what the life in Christ is all about. He gives no prescription that moving into this more vibrant walk with Christ comes from a mechanical tool kit that has a "no-fail guarantee."

In these pages, Doug reveals the depths of his personal struggle with power and clarity. You will feel it with him. More importantly, he walks us through a guided process of discovery to a new reality. It is a "Mission Possible," not an unattainable hope. We know that no human book changes lives. But it can guide us to experience a renewed relationship with Christ that is truly transforming.

I have seen the impact in Doug's life. It is the real thing.

JERRY WHITE, PhD
Major General, U.S. Air Force, Retired
International President Emeritus, The Navigators

ACKNOWLEDGMENTS

This book is a gift from my family to you. My wife endured increased responsibilities and fewer weekends together for nearly two years while I was buried in my office writing. She suffered through reading many early versions of the book, and she has diligently prayed for you and me. My son Jason kept me on message when I began to stray into the many subpoints of the book that could have become books in themselves. His passion to get this book to his generation encouraged me greatly. The editorial review, feedback, and support of Justin, my son-in-law, were enormously helpful. My daughter, Jennie; my son Matt; and my daughters-in-law, Katie and Kayla, amazed me with their prayer, encouragement, and input. Our whole family has its heart and soul in this message and is eager for you to encounter God in a far richer and more exciting way.

Next, I want to acknowledge the mentors in my life who have propelled my walk with God. The first and longest-running mentor is Jerry White, former president of The Navigators and now Chairman of the Board. He is a hero of mine and has represented the King of kings well in every arena of life. I only hope I can follow somewhat closely in his steps. Steve Blomquist, while a senior at the U.S. Air Force Academy, invested heavily in this young cadet. Dr. Howard Hendricks helped me navigate life during seminary days and provided my early introduction to the broader Christian community. Finally, I want to thank pastor Jimmy Siebert of Antioch Community Church in Waco, Texas, who has inspired me with his walk with God and challenged me to go further than I would ever have gone on my own.

Terra McDaniel, the development editor of *More Than Ordinary*, endured countless revisions of this book and poured over every sentence to ensure the words flowed well and the message was authentic. Even amid losing her home and possessions to a tragic fire, she tirelessly dedicated eighteen months, nearly full-time, to helping me refine and clarify this life message and make it relevant to a postmodern world. She and her husband, Kyle—who also contributed incredible support and wisdom— aspire to walk with God in the same way that Jan and I aspire to, and they have sacrificed a lot to see this book in print.

Two editors with NavPress provided significant input. Connie Willems helped in the early stages with the structure. Sue Kline fulfilled the major editorial work and did an amazing job.

Several authors have profoundly shaped my thinking, including A. W. Tozer, John Piper, Norman Geisler, Frank Laubach, John Calvin, C. S. Lewis, and J. I. Packer. While I have quoted some of them in this book, their thoughts have echoed in my head for years. I hope they would be pleased with their personal impact on me.

Navigator board member D. G. Elmore prompted me to get this book published. I am also deeply grateful for publisher

Mike Miller, who saw a collection of raw material and recognized that it could strengthen Christians around the world to walk with God all the days of their lives.

Last, I want to thank our friends at The Journey Church in Little Rock, Arkansas, who endured the early versions of this book in teaching and mentoring. Their encouragement, prayer, and feedback have been invaluable.

INTRODUCTION

This is a story that has been forty-six years in the making. It started the day I met a stranger in my backyard, and it's far from over. It's a story about discovering a God who is very different from the cold, stoic disciplinarian many of us heard about when we were kids. It's about discovering a life that is never boring.

> Go to www.morethanordinary.org to view videos, read Doug's blog, download additional tools, and join the More Than Ordinary team.

I'll understand if you're skeptical. You probably find the lives of most religious people pretty underwhelming. Jesus may have promised joy and abundance, but how many people do you know who actually live that way?

I'm writing to you as a businessman, husband, and father with the same kind of conflicting demands and priorities that you have. I head to the office every morning to start a hectic day. I'm away from home on business more than I'd like. I wish I had more of myself to give to my family. I sometimes struggle to make ends meet.

In the middle of this real world, I've learned to enjoy God. I want you to experience that too. And I want you to know from the start that I'm not going to tell you to add more tasks to your already overloaded to-do list. God intended us to enjoy Him right in the middle of the lives we're already living.

Some of you like to know where you're headed when you open a new book. Here's how it'll play out: We're going to look at God as if for the first time. What makes Him God? What makes Him captivating? Why did He bring you into the picture, and what kind of life does He want to have with you? The answers will lead you to end your typical day with some very atypical stories of encountering and enjoying God.

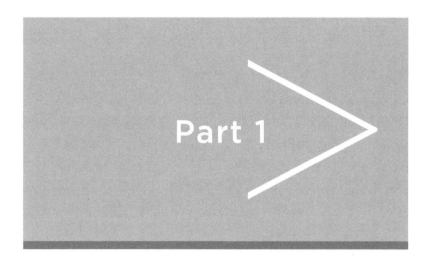

Part 1

ENCOUNTERING
GOD

CHAPTER ONE

A DIFFERENT WORLD

Encountering a real Person

On a bitterly cold day in the final year of World War II, a young American B-17 bomber pilot led his squadron on a raid deep into Nazi Germany. It was the last raid he would fly. Returning from the mission, three of his four engines were destroyed by anti-aircraft artillery. With all hope lost of making it back to the base in England, the pilot was forced to ditch the plane in the Nazi-occupied Netherlands. He and his crew were immediately captured.

That pilot—my father—spent the next seven months in a prisoner-of-war camp. No Allied prisoners were treated well, but my father was singled out for intensified attention because he was a Jew. The German Secret Service interrogated him regularly.

One of the Nazi rituals was deeply damaging to my father. He had always hated bombing civilian targets. Now, as a prisoner of war, he was routinely marched with other pilots through towns that had been destroyed by Allied bombers. The fury of the townspeople and the humiliation dished out by the Nazi guards left wounds that few men in their early twenties were equipped to handle.

Near the end of the war, recognizing that defeat was imminent, Hitler ordered all prisoners of war to be assembled into a single camp of seventy-five thousand Allied airmen and soldiers. Then he ordered the guards to line the perimeter of the camp with machine guns and open fire. This, my father thought, was the end. But there was a glitch: The prison guards didn't have enough ammunition to kill everyone. Rather than killing some and then having to face the wrath of the survivors, they simply stood watch over the prisoners until General Patton's tank entered the camp to liberate the cheering POWs. That was the remarkable end of my father's part in the war.

He met my mom, a Red Cross worker, at his next assignment. They were married and returned to the United States, where Dad settled into civilian life selling assembly-line tools to automakers in Detroit, northern Indiana, and Cleveland. We moved around a lot as he hopped from one company to another.

A volcanic rage rumbled inside my dad. His father had divorced his mom and left the family behind when my father was very young. That childhood rejection combined with the horrors of war fueled his anger, which was always close to the surface. He hated his boss, his job, his life. In many ways, he was still at war, but now the battle was coping with his uncontrollable rage. Home is where he vented all his accumulating frustrations. As far as I remember, the only variable in his attitude when he walked in the door after work was the *level* of his anger. As the oldest child, I was a lightning rod for his resentment and was his first target. Something about me always seemed to provoke him.

One evening when I was around seven years old, Dad had had enough of me ruining his return home from work, so he bent over to get eye level with me and placed his face, red with fury, a few inches from mine. He told me it was all he could do to restrain himself from bloodying me up. From now on, he said, I was to leave the house as soon as I saw his car pull up. He needed a few moments of peace before he had to suffer my presence. In the Indiana winter, leaving the house meant walking through snowdrifts on freezing windy nights. Indelibly etched in my memory is sitting on our split-rail fence listening to the wind howl while I stared into the brightly lit kitchen where my mother and father shouted at each other, fighting about me. I felt undesirable and unwanted. Home never felt like a safe place.

So I grew up in the dark shadow of constant worry, insecurity, and fear. His fist thrust in my face seemed to be my dad's main fathering tool. I can't remember if he ever let loose, but I lived in fear of that fist every day of my young life.

It won't surprise you that my dad and I didn't talk much unless he was criticizing or berating me. His words were more destructive than his physical threats. He constantly asked, "What's *wrong* with you?" with a look of disgust and his hands on his hips. When I was in elementary school, my hand-eye coordination matured more slowly than that of the rest of the kids, so when I played baseball, I usually either dropped the ball or missed it entirely. Dad was the most vocal of the spectators in the stands. Between innings, he would angrily demand, "Other kids can do it. Why can't you?" I was sure there *was* something wrong with me; I just didn't know what it was. I felt worthless and ashamed of myself.

When baseball did not go well, my mother saw to it that I became a Boy Scout. This led to the nearly inevitable interest in camping. What boy doesn't love knives, fires, hiking, sleeping outdoors, and merit badges? I immediately noticed that the other dads came to meetings and seemed to enjoy camping with their sons. I was one of only a few kids whose dad didn't participate. One afternoon I worked up the courage to ask him to come on the next camping trip. My question hung in the air as he thought about it. Finally, he said he'd had enough of sleeping outdoors during the war. I walked away dejected, convinced it wasn't the outdoors he'd had enough of; it was *me*.

Experiences such as these told me loud and clear how my father felt about me: *You disappoint and disgust me. You will never be anything but a screwup. You are strange, and I take no pride in you and have no joy in being with you.* He constantly reminded me how he looked forward to my eighteenth birthday when he could legally shove me out the door. I remember only one positive thing he said to me in all of my years at home: I had made a good tackle in a football game.

FIGHTING BACK

When I was fourteen, something in me snapped. I still desperately longed for my father's affection and approval, but I couldn't stand that he had such power over me. I hated myself for my lack of courage to take him on and keep him from venting his fury toward my mom and little brother. I resolved that I would no longer be his victim. Instead of fearing him, I would hate him. All my loneliness, hurt, and insecurity was turned into rage toward him. I dreamed of beating him up.

I was still too small—but one day it would be my fists in *his* face!

In the meantime, I started doing exactly what I wanted to do when I wanted to do it. My friends and I pursued the thrill of shoplifting—this brought momentary happiness and camara-derie—and drank beer when we could steal it from one of our homes. We went to school when and if we wanted to and did homework only when we felt like it—which was rarely. And I became the undefeated champion of our neighborhood's street fights. Other boys couldn't wait to test their strength against me as, week after week, I left some guy who stood up to me bloodied from a violent backlash.

Before long, a hard-nosed guy from the poorer side of town decided to pick a fight with me. His name was Ron. He was from a family with thirteen children and lived in a dilapidated house covered with peeling paint. His father was an auto mechanic, and their front yard was littered with disassembled old cars. I saw Ron wear only one set of clothes to school: a typi-cal sixties look of black pants, white shirt, black dress shoes, and white socks.

Ron started the fight, but unfortunately he caught me on a day when I was seething with resentment toward my dad. With a large crowd of boys and girls watching, he took the first swing. I ducked, and then in a fit of uncontrollable rage I rapidly punched him again and again in the face. I came through the fight unscathed, but I knew I had hurt him badly.

Ron did not return to school for several weeks. Each day he did not come back I felt worse. I was ashamed of myself. I worried he would drop out of school. Then I began asking myself the question I had heard all my life: *What is wrong with me?* Other kids didn't get into this kind of trouble. They weren't as cruel and violent as I was. I couldn't stop worrying about what I had done and who I was becoming.

What I thought was freedom had backfired. The more I did what I wanted, the more miserable I was. It was obvious I was headed toward jail or some other catastrophe, and I was very afraid.

FIRST ENCOUNTER

About a week later, something happened that would change my life forever. On a crisp November day in 1964, I was slumped on the old brick steps behind our home in a suburb of Cleveland, thinking about how my new life strategy was a colossal failure. The once vibrant leaves littered the yard—dull, brown, wet, and depressing. The barren trees, ugly against a wintry gray sky, matched my mood.

As I looked at the dismal landscape, the thought occurred to me out of nowhere that God had the answers I needed. I didn't know a single person who acknowledged God. No one talked of God or the meaning of life in my home. Dad, though Jewish by background, was an avowed atheist with great contempt for most religions, especially Christianity. Mom did not talk about spiritual things either but did mention Jesus' birth at Christmas. None of my friends were religious. I had been taught a few songs in Hebrew at a Jewish summer camp but couldn't remember what the words meant. Yet without any external guidance, something told me there must be a God somewhere who could help me.

My wandering thoughts about God were interrupted by a sight that took my breath away. I felt as if I were dreaming, but I knew what I saw was real.

A Man appeared and walked up to me. No introduction was needed. It was Jesus. I can't explain how I knew, but I *knew*. When God reveals Himself, He doesn't need a lot of fanfare or explanation. He can't be mistaken for anyone else. Jesus was tall and regal with olive-toned skin and dark hair that fell past His ears. His friendly face showed concern for me. But what riveted my attention were His eyes. They were dark, kind, and could look right through me. I felt completely exposed yet not condemned. He saw the things I was ashamed of but didn't look at me with disgust.

I already knew I was dying inside. Now I knew Jesus had come to rescue me. I was deeply moved that He had pursued me! As though pushed from behind to say something, I cried out, "Jesus, I have made a mess of my life. Would You *please* take it and run it for me?" With my cry echoing in the darkness, the image vanished, and my yard came back into focus. But though I couldn't see Him anymore, I knew Jesus was still present with me.

For the rest of the day I was dizzy with emotion. I felt clean on the inside and strangely warmed by Jesus' affection. A huge load had lifted, and I knew He was running things now. Perhaps for the first time in my life I had hope of a better existence.

The next morning, I bounded down the stairs for breakfast with new energy and an uncharacteristic smile. My mother raised her eyebrows, grinned, and said something like, "Who are you and what have you done with my son?" Six years later, she found out firsthand when she too met Jesus.

GROWING COMPANIONSHIP

As I began my first full day with Him, I already had some strong impressions about Jesus. I could tell He was not an idea or a distant spiritual force but a real Person with thoughts, feelings, and a personality. I sensed that He liked me and enjoyed my company. From the beginning, I had an amazing and nearly continual awareness that He was with me in every activity.

>> From the beginning, I had an amazing and nearly continual awareness that He was with me in every activity. Here I was, an insecure fourteen-year-old, struggling with feeling worthless, ashamed to be taking up air in my dad's presence. And now I was being confronted with the idea that the Creator of the universe was sitting next to me and actually liked being with me. >>

My family lived about a mile from school. As I walked to campus that day, the world seemed different because Jesus was walking with me. Delight filled the vacuum in my heart. It seemed natural to want to talk with Him.

It was as if I was seeing the world around me for the first time. The trees and sky amazed me on that walk as it struck me that Jesus created those and all things. I felt an impulse to tell Him how great He is, and so I did. The birds, squirrels, clouds, and even the cold air were all conversation starters. The more I admired Him and noticed how wonderful and active He is in everything, the happier I was. Just saying "Thank You, Jesus" for something brought fresh life and joy.

A fundamental shift in my outlook on life began that day. My first class was biology. I hated the subject and didn't like the teacher much either. If I went to class at all, you could count on me to make trouble. But the clear sense that Jesus was sitting next to me now changed everything. A new impulse occurred: the desire to please Him with my approach to school. Without any input from Him, I just knew I should pay attention.

We opened our textbooks to a picture of a cell. My teacher began explaining its components and operations in the monotonous tone of someone who'd covered that chapter a hundred times. But as I listened, a light dawned. The Person sitting next to me was the Creator of the substructure of all living things! Throughout the lecture, I sat in silence and admired Him.

Here I was, an insecure fourteen-year-old, struggling with feeling worthless, ashamed to be taking up air in my dad's presence. And now I was being confronted with the idea that the Creator of the universe was sitting next to me and actually liked being with me. This idea arrested my thoughts although I doubt I could have explained it to anyone at the time.

In the coming months, the level of pleasure in this companionship grew. As we walked to school together, I talked to Jesus about my friends and my feelings about life. I had a sense He listened to every word with concern and an interest in mentoring me. When I took a test, I would ask Him to help me remember what I had studied or even to help me when I had not studied. Sometimes the answers came and sometimes, when I had been too lazy to prepare, I sensed Him letting me sweat it out. I knew He was on the field with me when I played sports. I experienced the privileged existence of facing every challenge— and there were plenty—*with Him.*

Then, a few months after my first encounter with Jesus, I went to a friend's house on a Saturday night and did not think of Jesus once during the evening. I did not talk to Him, listen to Him, or consider how to please Him. When I returned home,

I felt a sinking sensation in my stomach. It was as if I had left my Friend at home and gone to have fun without Him. I felt rude for not including Him and also empty. It just wasn't the same without Him. I had become so accustomed to enjoying His company throughout the day that not to experience it felt like a real loss. That night I apologized and then lay awake marveling at His kindness and graciousness toward me. Unlike my dad, He didn't seem grumpy or disgusted.

Some people get to learn what God is like through the example of fathers who represent Him well. Others, like me, learn to appreciate what He is like by the contrast with their human father. Jesus always seemed to desire what was best for me. He was for me and loyal to me even when I let Him down.

ADVENTURE

After school on the second day of Jesus' coming to live with me, I felt an inexplicable impulse to go into my basement. The old family memorabilia stored there was always interesting to go through when my parents were away. But this was more than curiosity. I felt I should look for something specific although I didn't know what. As I rummaged in an old cardboard box, I discovered a Bible my mother had been given as a child. The pages were stuck together as if it had never been opened. I was certain God had led me to this discovery and felt as if I had won the lottery!

Gingerly, as though handling a great treasure, I carried the book upstairs and set it on my bed. I remembered a painting I had seen, maybe in an art class, of an old man on his knees reading the Bible. So I got on my knees. I let the Bible flop open to whichever page gravity directed. I read a little and then talked to Jesus about what I had read. *What does this mean? Why did You do that? Why did the people act that way? Is this really what You are like? Are You really this wonderful?* I read and studied the Bible on my knees this way, in a running dialogue, until I finished high school.

One day before school, I got up early to kneel in front of my bed as usual to talk with Jesus about the Bible. Suddenly my dad opened the door to my bedroom. When he grasped what I was doing, he exploded with a long string of expletives. He accused me of being weak and effeminate. He said I'd never become a real man if I continued on this course. I said nothing but stayed on my knees with a resolve that I would not let him rob me of my conversation with Jesus.

We stared at each other for maybe twenty seconds, but it seemed like hours. Remarkably, my dad did not snatch the Bible from my hands, but he slammed the door and left a terrible feeling in the room. From that point on, his disgust for me only grew.

Once my father stormed away, I returned to reading, asking Jesus to help me. Again, I let the Bible flop open to a page. I read with amazement a passage that spoke about how following Jesus sometimes puts you in conflict with those who do not love Him. I was overwhelmed that He had encouraged me so directly, speaking with power and clarity right into a situation I was facing. I realized that something inside of me had changed. How Jesus saw me and felt about me was becoming vastly more important than how Dad saw me.

The whole world seemed full of God's direct and personal work. If I made a sports team, got a date with a pretty girl, or received a compliment from a teacher, I saw God's hand in it. As the weeks passed, I recognized His handiwork in nature, in science and history courses, and in the ways He helped me at home. Lying in bed at night, I wondered what the next day would hold with Jesus. What flashes of power would I see? What would He whisper to me? What would we talk or laugh about together? I began to wake up with optimism and excitement, knowing He was in the room with me, eager for us to walk together. I entered into every day with a sense of adventure.

Don't get me wrong. All my problems didn't go away after I met Jesus. My dad's anger continued to boil. And I still had all the worries of a typical teenage boy: the stress of school, insecurity about girls, and fears of not making the football or wrestling team. But I was walking with a God who was so wonderful that I could find joy in knowing Him no matter what was happening around me. He seemed to tower over all my problems. My life was vastly better because of Him.

BEYOND ORDINARY

Whenever I describe my first years with Jesus, someone nearly always compliments *me*, as if I were more gifted or insightful than most. Nothing could be further from the truth. The story I have to tell is not about what a great teenager I was but about the great God I met. It was His character and nature that changed me from the inside out. *And He desires to do the same for you!*

I've had the privilege of speaking before large groups of people at churches and Christian organizations, and the even greater honor of mentoring individuals to walk with God in a way similar to what I learned in high school. And I have seen firsthand that the life I've been describing is not the experience with God most people sustain throughout their lifetimes.

Too many people miss seeing God as friendly, active, relevant, and interested in their daily circumstances. I've mourned that so few people return home at the end of the day with stories about the experiences and challenges they just faced *with* God. My guess is that if I were to ask most people, "Of all the extraordinary experiences you've had with Jesus today, which was the best?" I would get blank stares or maybe puzzled smiles. They can't imagine God showing up on an ordinary day and making it amazing. They can't fathom a God who wants them to be filled with joy, pleasure, and excitement and to live lives that are anything but commonplace.

>> I have seen firsthand that the life I've been describing is not the experience with God most people sustain throughout their lifetimes. >>

I'll never forget an attorney who had been to seminary but then switched to law. After hearing me speak, he went home and told his family that despite years of training and church involvement he never heard anyone talk about life with Jesus as an adventure. The life modeled for him was a lot like being a Boy Scout. The focus was on being a moral person and fulfilling a long list of religious dos and don'ts rather than enjoying God in any tangible way. He would describe his life with God, he said, as boring and flavorless yet responsible and dutiful.

I have come to realize over the years that to have been grounded in who God is and what life with Him is like *before* entering the modern religious establishment was a great gift. Throughout high school, when I was getting to know God, I never had contact with another Christian, heard no sermons from the Bible, and had no spiritual mentor. All my spiritual development occurred from personal encounters with God in the Bible and in my life experiences. I call this a gift because I was protected from the tragically low expectation of what life with God can be that permeates a great deal of Western Christianity. It never occurred to me that there might be a ceiling to what is possible with Him. It never occurred to me that I could encounter God only through quiet times or church services or serving the poor. Please understand that I am not denigrating any of these practices; they are all important elements of a lifelong walk with God. But they are not the sum total of what that walk is about. God has so much more He wants to give us!

Perhaps saddest of all, I've seen that it is all too ordinary for people to miss being touched personally by God's deep love, loyalty, greatness, power, and wisdom. After high school, about once a year for forty years until my dad died, he and I talked about Jesus' invitation for Dad to live an expansive, more than ordinary life with Him for all eternity. Dad's response to me, usually after hours of dialogue, was always something like this: "I see what you are saying and can't prove you wrong. But Jesus just doesn't move me." Like many, he believed that God probably exists and is good in an academic sort of way. But he would not let God become personal to him.

Many Christians are in a similar boat. Few are captivated by God or find their major source of joy in knowing Him. Few seem to find Him very interesting. Few have more loyalty for Him, more desire and passion to follow Him, and more joy in knowing Him today than they did a few years ago. Some start well in walking with God, but few live their entire lives with a growing zeal to know Him and make Him known.

I am absolutely convinced that what God has shown me isn't

just for me. *God's infinite desire is for you to engage Him every day in such a way that you enjoy a growing companionship and a great adventure and are fundamentally changed from the inside out by His incredible character.* This is the life God created you to live with Him, and He is devoted to giving it to you. He is relentlessly pursuing you for the kind of deep relationship I began with Him in high school. Your part is to respond to His initiation.

Maybe you're thinking this is too good to be true. You might be listening to condemning voices in your mind saying you could never have a life like this even if you tried. Maybe you are afraid that this kind of life with Jesus will be unbearably hard.

>> I've enjoyed periods of accelerated progress in living life with God, but I have also had seasons of going backward in my relation- ship with Him. >>

Soon I'll celebrate my forty-sixth year of walking with Jesus. During that time, I've enjoyed thirty-six amazing years of marriage to a wonderful woman, a tour as an Air Force instruc- tor pilot, and the founding and running of several businesses and nonprofits. Jan and I have raised three kids together. But like most people, I have faced significant trials. My family and I have endured financial crises. Friends and coworkers have betrayed me. I have sometimes carried the weights of discouragement and depression.

Amid all that, I've enjoyed periods of accelerated progress in living life with God. But I have also had seasons of going back- ward in my relationship with Him. I'll describe one of them in the next chapter. Sometimes difficulties have tempted me to mistrust God's motives or to count on my own ability instead of trusting Him. I've slumped into a mediocre existence from time to time, seemingly unable to live above my circumstances or to be captivated by and focused on God.

But I know one thing without a doubt. I have tasted the life He wants to give—and I want more! I want to experience everything God wants to give me in Him and to help others do the same. I am hungry for more of Jesus and determined to experience *all* God has for me.

Frank Laubach, a missionary to the Philippines in the 1930s, wrote in *Letters by a Modern Mystic*, "I feel convinced that for me, and for you who read, there lie ahead undiscovered continents of spiritual living compared with which we are infants in arms." I have poured my life into writing this book because I want you to explore such "undiscovered continents of spiritual living." Of course, your exploration won't be perfect. Sometimes it will be a matter of two steps forward and one step back. It will be hard at times, but no other way of living compares. It will cost you a lot, but it will be worth it. The apostle Paul said it better than I can: *"But just as it is written,* THINGS WHICH EYE HAS NOT SEEN AND EAR HAS NOT HEARD, AND *which* HAVE NOT ENTERED THE HEART OF MAN, ALL THAT GOD HAS PREPARED FOR THOSE WHO LOVE HIM *"* (1 Corinthians 2:9). God has more amazing things planned for you than you could possibly imagine, and I don't want you to miss any of it.

ENCOUNTERING GOD SUGGESTION

Turn your thoughts to Him a few times in the middle of the day, reminding yourself of His presence, His interest, and His loyalty. See how that changes your interaction with Him and how it changes the day for you.

CHAPTER TWO

THE LIFE GOD DESIGNED

Encountering a perfect Father

I was returning from an overseas business trip in December 2002. I had started a sales consulting company several years earlier that required a great deal of travel. When my plane landed in Little Rock, Arkansas—my family's home at that time—it was dark and cold outside, and I was exhausted. Even so, I stopped at the office after leaving the airport and knocked out several projects and a long line of e-mails that couldn't wait. I was eager to see my wife, so I finished as quickly as possible and headed home.

Briefcase in hand, I came in from the garage to the glow of the kitchen and a warm welcome from Jan. Her face, as always, told me she was happy to see me. She gave me a big hug and then pulled back so she could look into my eyes. Her penetrating dark brown eyes could always see right through me. "How did your day go?" she asked.

I looked at the floor and replied with sad resignation, "Well, I did not get done *all* that I wanted to get done today." With a gentle smile, Jan responded, "Do you know those have been your exact words every night for the last year or so when you've come home from work?" Her question hung in the air for a few seconds as the implications of her comment flooded my mind. I know she meant them as a gentle encouragement to trust God with my responsibilities, but her words cut like a knife.

I went into my home office and wept.

What had happened to me? It wasn't just that my description of my day was trivial and self-centered. I saw clearly, in that moment, that I had lost something very valuable: a close friendship with Jesus. The companionship and camaraderie I had with Him in high school and for most of my adult life had slowly evaporated. Gone was the excitement of waking to face the events of the day with Him, partnering with Him, enjoying life together. I was sickened by what a poor friend I had become to Him when He had been so unwaveringly loyal to me. I was responding to Him as if He were a distant King, not a close Friend. Life had become more about duty and keeping the rules than finding pleasure in knowing and following Him. I missed my Friend, and it hurt deeply.

I reflected on all the people I had urged over three decades to encounter Jesus as I had in high school. I felt I had let them down. I hadn't experienced just a single shallow day, but for an entire season, maybe a year or more, I had known that life felt wrong and my happiness was at low ebb. My response to Jan revealed volumes about what had become really important to me.

I lay awake that night wondering how my life had become so dull and gray. I thought I was doing the right thing by providing for my family, and at one level I was. But I had slowly become consumed with success and frustrations at work. I was spiritually sleepy, largely unaware of God's presence in the course of the day. Life felt like one big hassle. I was lonely and empty.

That there was no moral failure in my life was a pretty shallow victory. I was a lay leader in my church, teaching Sunday school and men's groups. Jan and I gave money to good causes. Our marriage was solid. I was still reading the Bible every morning. Our kids were all doing well, and our business was successful and run with integrity. To our close friends, I seemed at the pinnacle of spiritual maturity. But while the outside looked good, my heart and mind were missing something vital. The erosion was not on the outside but on the inside, and like most erosion, it had happened slowly, over time.

It was not just that I was living a lesser *life*; I was thinking less of Jesus. While I still knew Him to be good, wise, and powerful, He was no longer captivating or compelling to me. He was not my main source of joy. I had slowly and subtly started navigating decisions and priorities on my own, and God had shifted from being my center to being an accessory of my life. I knew I couldn't live that way another day.

A FRESH START

The next morning, I woke up early. Every day of my life since I began following Jesus, I have had to ask God for fresh starts after a bad attitude, an unclean thought, or a foolish thing I did. He has always gladly and freely given them. On this morning, I had to ask for a new beginning after a *season* of drifting. How could He not be disgusted with me? But there was no sense of condemnation or anger, only His happiness at giving me a new beginning. It was bittersweet. Regret mixed with gratitude at such undeserved affection and kindness.

I sat at my desk pleading to have my friendship back. I wanted a renewal and restoration of what was lost. What happened next was a miracle. Over the next few hours my study seemed flooded with a supernatural light as God renewed my love and loyalty to Him and gave me fresh biblical perspective for relating to Him as a close Friend who is real and present throughout the full range of life circumstances. That morning began an amazing process of renewal.

Over the next several months I started waking up earlier and eagerly going to my home office to study the Scriptures and interact with God. I wanted to start with a fresh slate and completely relearn who God is and discover the extraordinary life He desires us to live with Him. He took me much deeper in my understanding of truths that I had studied before and even taught. He showed me a bigger world, a better God, and a greater vision of life with Him.

I didn't mind the sleep I was missing to study God's Word and pray. Far from it! I couldn't get enough of these early morning encounters. I found myself saying over and over, "I had no idea!" The rest of this book is the fruit of that study and the result of God's reigniting my love for Him. I offer it to you in hope that you will enjoy Jesus in a richer and more exciting way that is far beyond the ordinary.

On that first morning, I opened the Bible to its first verse and sat in silent awe for several minutes. *"In the beginning God created the heavens and the earth"* (Genesis 1:1). All my thoughts were riveted on the word *God.* The Holy Spirit seemed to underscore His name and fill my mind with thoughts about His nature—thoughts that could absorb my attention for eternity. I thought of how casual I had been toward Him lately and how little wisdom, power, love, or greatness I had ascribed to His name. With tears in my eyes, I apologized for how little respect and gratitude I had shown Him. I resolved to become absorbed with God as never before for the rest of my life.

WHAT GOD IS LIKE

I was reminded again and again of a simple basic truth. God is not an anonymous force, a blob of power, or some great energy basic to all of life. Start reading Genesis—or anywhere else in the Bible for that matter—and a very different portrait emerges. He is a Person. He is the most relational Person who exists. He has personality, character, and a sense of humor. He pays attention, speaks, and listens. He works, He laughs, and He grieves. His delight in fathering His children is undeniable.

>> He is a Person. He is the most relational Person who exists. He has personality, character, and a sense of humor. He pays attention, speaks, and listens. He works, He laughs, and He grieves. His delight in fathering His children is undeniable. >>

The Spirit opened my eyes to see that I had not been relating to Him as a Person but as a cold and distant Deity. I had spent years telling others that we could learn a lot about how to relate to

God by thinking about how we'd interact with a good father and friend. I'd emphasized that it is one thing to agree academically that God is a real and present Person, and it is quite another to actually treat Him as if that's true. But I had fallen into living my days largely indifferent to His presence. I wrote in my journal the words *practical atheist* and found it unspeakably painful to recognize the truth of what I'd just written about myself. I was shocked at the independence that had grown in me over the last year or so. Clearly, I needed to reset my whole view of God.

Not long after this, I shared with a friend what I was learning and relearning about life with God. He was an elder of a large church and an active leader. To my surprise, he was unmoved by what I was saying. He told me, "Doug, I simply don't see God as an actual Person. I have no feelings for Him; I am not moved by worship music. But I do like living a moral life and helping my family be better people. Honestly, God seems pretty distant to me, but I like His principles for life and they are enough for me." My friend probably represents what a lot of us feel. But to think of God as existing somewhere far away and being only vaguely interested in the lives of His children would be to disagree with what He says about Himself on almost every page of the Bible. We were created to respond to a Person, not to a list of rules and principles.

I needed another reminder from God. While He is indeed a Person, He is neither fallible nor finite. He isn't like human parents who come together to create a child who will grow up to have similar strengths, length of life, and abilities to theirs. He isn't like a tree that drops acorns that may grow into trees larger and healthier than the first. And He is nothing like a wizard behind a curtain who pretends to be larger than life but is actually a lonely old man working hard to keep up the charade.

He is an eternal Creator and King. Every attribute He has, He has in limitless amounts. For example, consider His wisdom. God is *infinitely* wise. There is nothing He does not know, there is nothing He needs to learn, and He never wonders what is going on in any molecule in the universe. All of eternity will not be long enough to discover even a small portion of what He knows. The same is true for discovering the dimensions of His power, His love, His beauty, and every one of His attributes. As my eyes were opened with these renewed insights, I began to see that my unspoken fear of heaven being boring was ridiculous.

I wanted to anchor my mind around the idea of the limitless dimension of God's attributes, so I did a study on galaxies. A galaxy contains billions of stars, and there are billions of galaxies in the universe. I studied a great galaxy called the Sloane Great Wall. It is actually a supercluster of billions of galaxies that was discovered in 2003. Scientists estimate that the Sloane Great Wall is more than a billion light-years in length. Because light moves at 186,000 miles per second, I will let you do the math for how truly massive this supercluster is. But while the Great Wall is the largest known structure in the universe, it is only a tiny part—much less than 10 percent—of its total.

Comparing this supercluster to anything we know is like comparing God's wisdom, joy, and integrity to our own. Not that we don't have minds to think, hearts to experience wonderful emotions, or characters that desire to do the right thing, but the dimensions of God's attributes are infinitely beyond ours. My problem wasn't that I didn't accept that God is good, wise, and powerful. I never stopped believing those things. Rather, my grasp of the *dimension* of His attributes was far too small. My mental image of His greatness had become so small that it was choking the life out of me!

This opened the door for me to take an attribute of God, such as His power, and reflect on what infinite power is like. Then I thought of His compassion, devotion, sovereignty, and other attributes. As my mental image of Him grew, I began to see a more God-centered world where He towers above everything and is far better than I had ever thought.

LIFE AS IT'S MEANT TO BE

As I continued reading in Genesis, I was caught up in imagining life in the Garden of Eden, the home God created for the first humans. What kind of life would an infinitely wise, powerful, relational Person design?

Adam and Eve must have had a glimpse of the raw power and authority with which God runs the universe. They would have seen unspeakable beauty—a million times more captivating than Mount Everest or the Grand Canyon—and experienced some of the depth of the Creator's wisdom, loyalty, and sovereignty. Life in the garden must have been paradise, for life with God is the true meaning of paradise.

Not only did Adam and Eve experience jaw-dropping majesty, but they were also deeply loved and completely accepted. The more we admire a person, the more we want that person's approval and acceptance. Part of paradise was the steadfast affection of the God of the universe. What words could possibly express the honor of undeserved attention from a God who desired friendship with His creation? Imagine being told by Him that of the entire universe, you are His greatest possession. Adam and Eve were not lonely, did not know the feeling of being unloved, and never worried they were undesirable. They never had to struggle with insecurity because they lived with a God who could not have been more devoted to or pleased with them, His children.

God creates that which is good because He is good. Every good desire we have is because He made us like Himself. If you treasure time with your family and friends, if you have a deep longing for travel and adventure, if you enjoy accomplishing something noble and right, then you should know that all these desires come from our heavenly Father.

"God created man in His own image, in the image of God He created him; male and female He created them" (Genesis 1:27). God created Adam and Eve (and all their children) with desires for majesty, honor, significance, and deep relationships similar to His own. This is what it means to be created in His image. Paradise was the only place where all the desires He created within us could be perfectly satisfied. His plan was to fulfill each one of them in the context of relationship with Him.

As I pondered these things, an amazing thought occurred to me. I flipped to the last two chapters of the Bible to be reminded of how the story ends. I read,

> *Behold, the tabernacle of God is among men, and He will dwell among them, and they shall be His people, and God Himself will be among them, and He will wipe away every tear from their eyes; and . . . there will no longer be any mourning, or crying, or pain.* (Revelation 21:3-4)

I sat in awe as I realized that paradise wasn't only God's first thought for humanity, a dream He gave up when we rebelled against Him. It was His plan before He made the world, and He never changed His mind. Even though our skepticism of His good-ness gets in the way of what He wants for us, He has never stopped working to be reunited with us. He sent His own Son to make a way for Him to dwell with us again, ultimately restoring paradise.

God never wanted people merely to study or talk about the wonders of His presence and personality. He meant for us to know them as the first humans did. As I reflected on all that I was relearning at a deeper level, I wrote in my journal a series of foundational truths:

- He is good.
- His motives are always infinitely good.
- His thoughts toward us are infinitely good.
- His gifts are infinitely good.
- Everything God does is good—perfectly good.
- Every commandment is for our good and the good of others.
- Every proper response to God is vastly better than a selfish response.
- His plans are much better than ours, and His heart is much purer than ours.
- He is infinitely devoted to creating the greatest good for the most people over the longest period of time in the best way possible.

The incredible idea that God is devoted to give us His best lingered in my mind for an hour or so. I wondered, *What would it be like to live fully confident that He will never waver in His devotion to me, never stop being loyal to me, or never fail to do what is perfect for me? What if all my subtle and unacknowledged suspicions about Him being cruel or capricious at times were bold lies?*

Then I thought about how far life today is from the life He designed. Things are not at all as God intended them to be.

He never wanted death, disease, pollution, crime, or sadness. He did not invent boredom, fear, anger, or insecurity. He despises injustice. He does not want anyone to hurt. He hates poverty, corruption, and disaster. God will tolerate these things only for a very small portion of eternity and will ultimately use all things for good. Somehow, every good and bad thing on the planet is being woven into His perfect plan. None of us can fully understand the depth of His wisdom in this. But one day, much sooner than you think, He will eagerly destroy all pain and evil so that His children can live with Him forever. He will enjoy us and we will enjoy Him through all eternity.

>> What would it be like to live fully confident that He will never waver in His devotion to me, never stop being loyal to me, or never fail to do what is perfect for me? >>

WHY DID GOD WANT CHILDREN?

I could clearly see that the life God intended for us was unspeakably wonderful. But could He stay devoted to us even when our first parents ruined paradise with their sin? I was bombarded by a string of questions, but at their heart was a very personal concern. What I really wanted to know is whether God endures my presence out of obligation and with bitterness like my dad.

Before I could go any further, I had to review what I knew to be true of God. I remembered that *"our God is in the heavens; He does whatever He pleases"* (Psalm 115:3). He cannot be coerced to do anything. I was thunderstruck: If God is not obligated to stick with us, then that means life with us is an essential part of His idea of paradise. Paradise is not just paradise for us; it is paradise for Him! He does only what pleases Him, and it clearly pleases Him to be with us and to father us. Up until that point, I had considered only what *we* got out of relating to Him, never what pleasure *He* received. But knowing that He enjoys fathering me this much makes relating to Him far more enjoyable for me.

But how could a God this perfect actually enjoy being with us? I wrote in my journal, "Lord, why did You want children in the first place?" I had never thought to ask this question before, and it was a doorway into very rich truth for me. We can get some of our greatest insight into God by learning what He enjoys.

While I wanted to have children in my early twenties, I was clueless as to what it would be like. God, on the other hand, knew exactly what fathering us would entail, and He still chose to create us and spend eternity with us.

When Jesus came to show us firsthand what God is like, He made clear by His teaching and example that God is by nature a *Father* who finds infinite delight in fathering His children even when they stray from Him. Jesus referred to God as Father more than two hundred times during the three years of His public ministry. The whole nature of Jesus' own relationship to God is described in the Gospels as that of a Son to His Father. The first words He taught us to pray are *"Our Father who is in heaven"* (Matthew 6:9). He said to His followers, *"If you then, being evil, know how to give good gifts to your children, how much more will your Father who is in heaven give what is good to those who ask Him!"* (Matthew 7:11).

I saw more clearly than I ever had that God did not have children out of need but because He wanted to. God doesn't need anything. He certainly didn't have a gap in His life; He was not lonely or needy. He was eternally content in community with

His Son and the Spirit. And because He knows all things past, present, and future, God wasn't surprised when Adam and Eve fell. He knew the corruption, havoc, and destruction that they would choose. Yet He created us, knowing what it would cost Him, *because He wanted to share His life and joy with us.* This was a better thought of Him than I had ever considered. I will spend the rest of eternity discovering the full depth of this truth!

It helped me grasp the nature of God's love of fathering us when I looked into my own heart and saw what I loved about parenting my three children. Analogies filled my head even though my delight pales in comparison to His. Here are a few insights I gleaned from my thinking. I hope they will help expand your image of Him as they did mine.

God Loves Our Company

The first memory I recalled was a camping trip with my boys to New Mexico when they were eight and six. One morning after breakfast, my younger son, Matt, wandered off to a big rock by the stream near our campsite. He sat there alone with his back to me. I put down the frying pan and sat next to him as he threw stones in the water. I put my arm around him, and we remained like that for several minutes. He didn't say anything, but when he looked up at me with his brown eyes shining, words can't express the delight I felt in being a father to him. It was pure joy to know that he loved being fathered by me.

Yet my joy that day must be miniscule compared to God's joy in engaging us in fellowship. The psalmist says it simply and powerfully: *"For the LORD takes pleasure in His people"* (Psalm 149:4). Just as He did with Adam or Eve, our heavenly Father loves to talk to and listen to us.

To say that God enjoys being with us in a similar way that I love being with my children doesn't mean that He agrees with every decision we make. Sometimes what we do makes Him grieve for what we are missing with Him. But His love never wavers. Nothing we do can make Him love us more, and nothing we do can make Him love us less. A perfect Parent will love His children through foolish, immature, and even rebellious decisions. This truth about God's passion for fellowship with me made me want to know Him better and follow Him more closely.

God Loves Planning Every Detail of Our Days with Him

When my kids were young, we regularly went camping, and I loved planning all the exciting and challenging experiences we would share. I was very deliberate about where we would camp, what food we would pack, and what gear we would need. I have to admit that planning these trips was always a little bittersweet for me; I would have loved this kind of interaction with my own father. But it was utter joy to give my children what I hadn't had myself.

In the same way, God plans every element of every day for us. He loves preparing the way for us to walk with Him and to experience the joys and disappointments of life with Him. The prophet Isaiah expressed this truth about God's intimate planning and involvement in every single detail of our lives when he said, *"O LORD, You are my God; I will exalt You, I will give thanks to Your name; for You have worked wonders, plans formed long ago, with perfect faithfulness"* (Isaiah 25:1). This truth forever changed the way I see my circumstances. I came to view every meeting, project, and conversation I had as an opportunity to see His hand, respond to Him, and enjoy Him. Knowing He would weave the results of each day into His perfect plan and that He would help me with every challenge brought me great peace and confidence.

God Loves to Bring Joy to His Children

When Jason was eight, Matt six, and Jennie one, the highlight of my day was arriving home from work. I would open the door to small voices yelling, "Daddy's home!" Quick as a flash, three smiling faces would round the corner into the hallway. Tossing aside my coat and tie, I would get on all fours, growling. The boys would jump on me, and we would spend the next hour wrestling, tickling, chasing, and laughing. Jason was the boldest and loved to be tickled. Matt usually approached more cautiously and then ran away laughing. And Jennie just giggled at the whole scene. I will let you guess whether it was the kids or me that got the most out of this daily ritual. We don't wrestle anymore now that they're adults, but I still take great delight in being with them.

One of the greatest desires of godly parents is to enjoy the affection, appreciation, and devotion of their children. God feels the same way. My passion to love my children well and bring them joy helped me get just a glimpse of what is in God's heart when He looks at me as His child. How could we not respond with great loyalty to One so loyal and devoted to us!

God Loves to Mentor His Children

When I was growing up, my two favorite sports were wrestling and football. I continued both in college. But as much as I enjoyed training and competing, I loved coaching my boys even more. I loved helping them discover secrets of how to win that no one else would tell them. I loved cheering for them at games and encouraging them about their performances. I loved watching Jennie dance and giving her tips on competing well. Seeing my kids win was better than winning myself!

Now that my children are grown, I still love helping them with things such as buying houses, handling work challenges, parenting, and making career decisions. I want my kids to experience the best life possible, and that's what God wants for us too. He is always working to help us reach our potential and not miss any good things He has planned for us. Unlike me, He is a perfect Father. He always has our best interests at heart. He promises us, *"I will instruct you and teach you in the way which you should go; I will counsel you with My eye upon you"* (Psalm 32:8). Knowing this makes me want to seek His counsel and His leadership more often.

God's eternal desire to dwell with us and to father us has vast, life-changing implications. I am drawn to know and follow a God like this. The more I reflect on what He is like, the more I want to know and please Him and the more I desire to walk with Him and enjoy life with Him. He is not a grim Father who suffers our presence and barely tolerates us. He is the polar opposite of my dad's worst attitudes when he got angry. The price God paid so we could live together with Him for all eternity only magnifies the image of His delight in His children.

RETURNING TO PARADISE

My exploration in the first two chapters of Genesis made me realize how much I had forgotten about God. Now I was remembering how the greatest moments of my life occurred when I was fully alert to God's presence and activity, experiencing His personality and character, filled with joy in knowing Him, and excited about what He would do next.

God is not distant or grumpy. He isn't a disgruntled moral policeman who can't wait for me to make a mistake so that He can write me a ticket and collect a fine. He is not a divine employer wanting me to set my alarm earlier so I can add even more duties to my work for Him. He is not a divine professor trying to fill my head with biblical information as if knowing the facts could change my life. He is a perfect Father whose intention for me has always been that I enjoy the life Adam and Eve had before the Fall. He is devoted to giving paradise to His children for all eternity. This view of God changes my lens for life.

I saw again that living consistently in God's presence in every event is the best life possible. I understood that the greatest gift is to see Him as He really is and to live with Him as Adam and Eve had. I remembered that every good response to Him is vastly better than ignoring Him or responding poorly. I realized anew the life God wants for all His children, and I didn't want to miss any of it with Him.

>> I resolved that the main question of my life would be this: Of all the paradise God desires to give me today, how much will I actually enjoy? >>

I don't know about you, but this is some of the best news I've ever heard. With my heavenly Father, I would never be on a fence in the cold, rejected because He was disgusted with me and tired of my presence. I would never have to beg God to spend time with me or to do things with me. In that season of study, I made a decision. *I resolved that the main question of my life would be this: Of all the paradise God desires to give me today, how much will I actually enjoy?* Thankfully, I've never had to depend solely on my resolve. God is relentless in His pursuit of every one of His children. He is always drawing us to experience more paradise every day until we have it fully in heaven.

I had not forgotten, however, how my connection and experience with God had fluctuated in recent years. I still needed insight into what makes it so hard to pursue Him over a lifetime. As I moved into the third chapter of Genesis, I found some answers for why we aren't living the life He meant for us. I grieved as I read the tragedy of how our first parents were tricked into doubting the God who had given them everything. The next chapter is about what was lost and how we lost it. More important, it is about how it was found again.

ENCOUNTERING GOD SUGGESTION

What would change in your response to God if you could live fully confident that He will never waver in His devotion to you, never stop being loyal to you, or never fail to do what is perfect for you? Talk to Him about any subtle and unacknowledged suspicions about Him being cruel or capricious at times. Ask Him to forgive you for believing lies about His character.

CHAPTER THREE

PARADISE LOST AND FOUND

Encountering a powerful Rescuer

God had started my season of renewal by reminding me of who He is and has been from the beginning of time. As the perfect Father, He designed a life for humanity that was infinitely wise. His plan was to give us His best gifts and the greatest possible experience with Him, and His motives were utterly pure. Everything about life in the garden was crafted to bring joy and fulfillment to both God and His people. But He is not the kind of God who would force us to live with Him or love Him, even though the alternative is incredibly tragic. Part of His perfect plan was giving His children the freedom to respond with either trust or doubt.

In that place of freedom a dark figure entered the story. The Devil, also called Satan, is the father of everything bad and broken, from sex slavery to genocide. His purpose in the garden was pure evil, and his plan was to use God's gift of freedom against God and the children He loves. Taking the form of a serpent, Satan convinced Eve that God was holding out on her and Adam by prohibiting them from eating from one tree in the garden. He tricked her into believing she could not fully understand God and His ways except by comprehending the contrast between good and evil. God was failing to give her all He could as her Father, Satan reasoned, and therefore she should reject His leadership.

The truth was very different from what Satan presented. God's commandment was not intended to deprive Adam and Eve. It was intended to protect them from the knowledge of evil that would bring hell on earth. It was like a father telling his children not to experiment with heroin, knowing that trying such a thing even once would be destructive. Every commandment God has ever given has been for our good—to give us the best life we could have and to protect us from harm.

TRAGEDY INVADES PARADISE

In an instant, Adam and Eve's decision changed their life in paradise with their loving Father. They made a subtle but significant shift from fully trusting their Father to putting more weight on their own understanding. They concluded they could find life on their own terms. But things didn't turn out the way Satan had made Adam and Eve believe they would. They knew immediately that rather than becoming more like God, they had lost everything. They felt an emotion they'd never experienced before. Shame compelled them to hide behind trees from the God they had always run to embrace.

>> We were created to do the best thing for us. We will act in self-interest. It is a God-given instinct, and it's right for us to think this way. The question is, will we believe what God, our Creator, says is best for us? Or will we reject the truth and adopt the flawed view that we've found a better way? >>

My eyes filled with tears as I read how our parents responded to the God who had given them life. I kept saying to Jesus, "Lord, what did we do? How could we have been so foolish?" Then, a powerful truth hit me with amazing clarity. In the tragic decision of Adam and Eve, I saw the pivotal point of human existence and the main strategy of Satan's evil, daily plan. In any given moment, our response to God is based on what we believe deep within ourselves about Him. Does He have our best interests at heart? Is it really best for us to respond well to Him? Is it such a big deal if we don't? The moment any of us waver in confidence that the answer to all these questions is a resounding yes, we make the same dark choices as Adam and Eve. Doubting His character and commitment leads to taking over our life on our terms, trusting our own wisdom over His. People respond to God with indifference and independence or love and loyalty based on their conclusions about His character and power in any given moment.

It boils down to this: We were created to do the best thing for us. We *will* act in self-interest. It is a God-given instinct, and it's right for us to think this way. The question is, will we believe what God, our Creator, says is best for us? Or will we reject the truth and adopt the flawed view that we've found a better way? The choice is whether to be God-led or self-directed. Every person will follow one of these two paths in any given moment or over a lifetime.

People do not walk with God over a lifetime because they ought to but because they are convinced that it is a privilege and that the alternative is not just slightly inferior but *much* worse. A general moral mandate to become better fathers, mothers, friends, and so on won't motivate the human heart over the long haul. Merely responding to a list of moral guidelines in lieu of engaging an amazing God leads to a boring, burdensome, and defeated life.

In the weeks before my conversation with Jan on that cold December night, I had been wondering why I didn't engage God more during the day. I knew that thinking of Him always made a moment better, so why wasn't I doing it more often? Why had it suddenly become such hard work to enjoy Him? As I reflected on Adam and Eve's decision, the answers to those questions became inescapably clear. Until I was convinced that responding well to God was a great exchange for me personally, I was always going to be tepid in my response to Him. The same is true for everyone. Unless we are increasingly convinced that God is passionate about our best interests and that every good response to Him is vastly better for us than living independently, we will not sustain loyalty to Him over a lifetime.

The game-changing truth is that because God is good, wise, and perfect in all things, *every proper response to Him is a monumental trade up.* Please read that sentence again because it has the power to change the way you live the rest of your life. Every time we choose to respond to God, we make the best possible choice because He is infinitely wise and abundantly loving. He knows the alternatives and gives us the best both for us and for those who live and work with us. Every right response to the Father has results that ripple outward and will be enjoyed for all eternity.

>> The game-changing truth is that because God is good, wise, and perfect in all things, every proper response to Him is a monumental trade up. >>

Over the next several weeks, and many times since, I reflected on God's promises and the truth that His ways, plans, gifts, and motives are indescribably better than mine. I realized anew that thinking of Him is far better than pondering my own goals and desires. This, in turn, caused me to want to think of Him more often. I could see that pleasing Him is much better than pleasing myself; this propelled me to ask Him more often how I could please Him. Remembering that His counsel and wisdom are brilliant and far superior to my own made me seek His direction more often.

I also began to pay attention to how easily I forget Him or begin to doubt Him. As I examined the state of my heart, I realized that my greatest sins weren't lust, envy, or anger but indifference and independence from God. I am often still stubbornly self-directed, but I follow Him more closely today than I did eight years ago because of what He taught me during this season. I learned firsthand that skepticism always puts relational distance between God and us. The same tired old lie that Adam and Eve believed—that God is not that devoted to us, loyal to us, or passionate about giving us His best—is the assumption that keeps people from knowing and following Him.

CONSEQUENCES THEN AND NOW

Once Adam and Eve had made their tragic choice, God could not allow them to stay in the garden. Even that was a kindness: They could not have survived in His presence in their fallen state. But separation from our Father is the worst tragedy imaginable. The horrors of earthquakes, tsunamis, cancer, and global poverty pale in comparison.

I don't believe Adam and Eve meant to leave God behind, but their choice to doubt His complete goodness made that unavoidable. Nothing they could do would return things to the way they'd been; they could not hear, see, understand, or relate to their heavenly Father as they once had. They must have felt very alone in the world, the way all of us would feel if we faced life's challenges without a Father and Friend. Life for our first parents was no longer filled with nobility, purpose, joy, and excitement because God was no longer at the center. The Bible calls this spiritual death.

Separation from God is the worst consequence of the tragedy in the garden, but it is not the only consequence. When Adam and Eve stopped seeing God clearly, they started seeing themselves, others, and their circumstances through a corrupt lens as well. The most ridiculous lies about God started making sense to them. Without knowing it, they began to let the father of lies—Satan—govern them. As the prophet Jeremiah would later mourn of their children's children, they began pursuing empty strategies: *"For My people have committed two evils: They have forsaken Me, the fountain of living waters, to hew for themselves cisterns, broken cisterns that can hold no water"* (Jeremiah 2:13).

Deceived by Satan's lies, Adam and Eve exchanged a life of

communing with God for *competing* with God. They claimed for themselves the place of honor and attention that only God deserves. Instead of submitting to God as their Maker and Sustainer, they placed themselves in the role of *judging* God and finding Him wanting. So they chose to control their own lives and ended up in a bondage to self-love stronger than any drug addiction.

From that point on, history records one tragedy after another as people began to live with little or no reference to God. Rather than expansive lives of celebration, they lived small lives marked by divorce, murder, incest, anger, fear, and all kinds of self-inflicted injuries. Reading Genesis after the third chapter isn't too different from watching today's news. Disease, death, injustice, pain, and the difficulty of work can all be traced to humanity's turning its back on God and concluding He wasn't good enough, attractive enough, or wise enough for their devotion.

As all this took shape during my study of Genesis, God also showed me something else about the results of the original sin. Christians can experience many of the same life consequences for indifference and independence toward God as those who don't know God: prolonged distance from Him, a distorted view of God and life, and many self-inflicted injuries. Although our response to Jesus' offer of salvation determines our eternal destiny, we still have a pretty good shot at ruining our lives if we choose to live as practical atheists with only a nominal interest in God.

The lingering effects of the Fall are still with us today. We naturally wake with a desire to compete with God for being God. Thankfully, the desire is not as strong as it was before Jesus came to live with us. But until we get home to heaven, a deliberate daily effort will be required to relinquish our urge to run things instead of trusting Him.

As I read about Adam and Eve, I begged God never to let me forget how much joy, adventure, pleasure, and significance is found in walking with Him. I asked Him to maintain a holy fear in me so that I wouldn't drift away from Him again. He was carefully revealing to me just how high the stakes are.

THE RESCUE

No good Father would sit idly by while His children suffered self-inflicted pain and misery. And God didn't. He sent His Son—the same Son who was with Him and the Holy Spirit when they created the world together—to restore us to Himself and to bring us home.

To rescue us from our ongoing separation from God, Jesus suffered a separation from His Father for the first time in eternity. He did the unthinkable because of love for His Father and love for us. He came to pay our ransom. He came to take upon Himself the justice that Adam, Eve, and every one of their children deserved for their unbelief and rebellion. One day, after a hard night of tears and sweat and agony, a friend's betrayal led to Jesus' arrest. He allowed Himself to be nailed to a piece of wood for the reward of seeing us experience the same Father-Child relationship He enjoys. It is what sustained Him through the agony of His horrific death. Hebrews 12:2 describes Him as *"Jesus, the author and perfecter of faith, who for the joy set before Him endured the cross, despising the shame, and has sat down at the right hand of the throne of God."* Jesus was thinking about *you* having a chance to know your Father as He was dying to make it possible. *We* were the joy set before Him!

Realizing that God was willing to sacrifice His beloved Son and be without His fellowship *for the first time in eternity* helps me imagine a little of the value God places on us. He loves us that much! We have forever to keep learning more of the answers to Paul's questions for the Romans: *"What then shall we say to these things? If God is for us, who is against us? He who did not spare His own Son, but delivered Him over for us all, how will He not also with Him freely give us all things?"* (8:31-32).

Our role in becoming children of God is simple. We trust His Son and the sacrifice He made to be enough, and then we devote our lives to enjoying Him and following Him. When we trust His leadership and His gift of forgiveness, we are adopted into the family of our Father. We receive the same kind of Fatherly love and devotion from God as He has for Jesus, although Jesus' position is rightly much greater than ours.

Once we become His, He considers us family and doesn't count our past against us. That's when the process of making our hearts and minds match His can begin. In the time between coming to know Him and getting to heaven, we have the chance to cooperate with His Spirit to make our character, will, and actions honor our Father. We get to participate with Him in bringing His kingdom to where we live. We get to follow Jesus' example in bringing heaven to earth.

And this only scratches the surface of the rescue Jesus provided for us. He rescued us *from* something: the eternal consequences of Adam's and Eve's and our own sin. But He also rescued us *for* something: a renewed relationship with our Father and a new promise of paradise.

And this rescue continues every day. Every day we need a Savior to rescue us from the effects of our indifference and independence. He is passionate about saving us from all that keeps us from experiencing the life He intends.

I believe most Christians are pretty clear on what they have been saved *from* but are foggy about what kind of life they have been saved *to* enjoy. They know we will go to heaven one day, but how we bring heaven to earth is less than clear. We know a lot about the duration of eternal life but little about the quality of what that life is supposed to be either on earth or in heaven.

WALKING TOWARD PARADISE

Becoming a child of God is the first step on a journey back to paradise. One day we'll be transported to heaven, where paradise will be full strength. But meanwhile, once Christ comes to live in us, we take the first step of many that allows us to experience more and more of the joy and adventure of paradise in our daily lives until we eventually reach the ultimate reality in heaven.

The Father, the Son, and the Holy Spirit move in with us; we wake every day to all three members of the Trinity. They live all of life with us, participating in everything we do. They are eager to rescue us from the things that keep us from the Father and to help us walk closely with Him every day in the midst of a sin-corrupted world. They open our eyes to the ways the Father is constantly revealing Himself to us through His Word, through creation, and in circumstances. And Jesus and the Holy Spirit continually pray for us to our listening Father. Not a moment of our lives is outside the care of the Father, Son, and Holy Spirit.

When we become children of God, our *position* is permanent and unchanging. But our relationship with Him grows and develops over time. Just as children have good and bad days with their parents, we'll have ups and downs with our Father. It is one thing to become a child of God and an entirely different thing to choose to respond to Him with love and loyalty on a daily basis.

In light of this process, this series of steps, it's no wonder the main scriptural metaphor for life with God is that of *walking* with Him (see, for example, Leviticus 26:12; Deuteronomy 5:33; 1 Kings 2:3; Romans 6:4; 2 Corinthians 5:7; Galatians 5:16). In Genesis, God commanded Abraham to walk before Him (see 17:1). In the first five chapters of the Bible, all people are called to walk in His ways. And in the New Testament, believers in Jesus are instructed to walk by following the Holy Spirit in what they say and do (see Romans 8:1-14), to walk in the light of God's presence and personality, and to walk in total surrender to His will (see Romans 6:11).

Walking with God is living each hour seeing and responding to Him through the wilderness of life circumstances. He wants His children to enjoy companionship and adventure and to be changed by His nature in the process. Walking with God involves taking specific steps and being led by a Person through the decisions and activities of the day.

>> Walking with God is living each hour seeing and responding to Him through the wilderness of life circumstances. >>

This includes every realm of life. It is not just what we do for a few minutes in the morning while reading our Bibles; it is actively and deliberately walking with God from Sunday morning through Saturday night. We can walk with God at a football game, during dinner with family or friends, and when something wonderful or terrible happens. He wants to empower us to live above all our circumstances and amid all our responsibilities and to be continually captivated by His majesty.

And here's something that is really important. It is just as vital—and possible—to engage God at work as it is at church. (This was the main point of my earlier book, *Your Work Matters to God*.) God wants to lead us and participate with us in *everything*, from what we say to our spouse to how we respond to our boss.

Sadly, most people have a very limited vision of walking with God. Many have been taught misguided notions about God. Some believe He's not interested in our messed-up world. Many people feel they're walking with God if they manage to stay away from major sins. Others seem to think walking with Him means engaging Him primarily in solitude; they believe they will be filled up and prepared for the majority of their active and public lives by an hour a day or a few weekends a year set apart for Him. Still others see walking with God as studying the Bible. Encountering the God of the Bible all day long doesn't occur to them.

But the worst conclusion I have seen people advocate is that walking with God is merely one profitable lifestyle option among many. They paint life with God as a wholesome, nice choice that is likely to yield a slightly better and more centered life. But Jesus made it clear that this life He offers immediately compels us, out of joy, to give up everything else. He said, *"The kingdom of heaven is like a treasure hidden in the field, which a man found and hid again; and from joy over it he goes and sells all that he has and buys that field"* (Matthew 13:44). When we see Him more clearly, we will pursue life with God with a consuming desire, a whole-hearted devotion, a willingness to pay any price because of the sheer value of the reward.

AN EPIC JOURNEY

As I was wrestling with this idea of walking with God, I told a friend how hard I was finding it to explain the full nature of what is at stake. He asked me if I had ever studied the Lewis and Clark Expedition as a metaphor for walking with God. I felt God was behind the suggestion, so I read a few history books on the subject. Then, not long after that, my son Matt and I had a chance to go on a guided wilderness adventure to retrace some of Lewis and Clark's route in Montana and Idaho with experts on the history of the expedition. We slept where Lewis and Clark slept, walked the same route, felt some of the hunger and exhaustion they experienced, and learned a lot about how God's miraculous hand guided them against seemingly impossible odds. While no illustration could possibly capture all the richness of a biblical concept like walking with God, I found many important parallels.

The results of Lewis and Clark's journey profoundly affected the history of the United States and even most of the free world. Their goal to find a water route from St. Louis to the Pacific allowed them to chart territory previously unknown to any but Native Americans. Their expedition opened the way for a young country to explore its resources and expand westward.

Progress was slow, and they made many mistakes. They didn't comprehend the dangers of the terrain or the wildlife they would encounter, such as a new species of bear. They didn't understand how to interact peacefully with the Native Americans they met. They nearly starved to death while camping next to streams brimming with salmon because they didn't know to look for them.

But what they saw and experienced was remarkable! Mountains and waterfalls of greater grandeur than they'd ever seen. Unexpected animals and amazing people whose customs were foreign to them.

Every day they woke up not knowing what would happen to them, but they pushed on. As Matt and I retraced their steps, we encountered trails so steep at times that all I could do was slowly put one foot in front of the other with my heart beating wildly and my lungs huffing and puffing. The original expedition had few paths to make its way easier and no modern instruments for navigation. Much of the drama the explorers faced revolved around whether they would follow their guide or trust their own instincts, putting them in peril.

They lived a far more significant and nobler life than those who merely read about the trip. For the rest of their lives, they were able to tell incredible true stories. They rightly received honor for what they achieved and what they sacrificed. They could be confident their lives counted for something bigger than their own interests. My friend was right. I could learn a lot about life with God by looking through the lens of an epic adventure like Lewis and Clark's.

A PRIVILEGED LIFE

Many men applied to accompany them on the journey, but Lewis and Clark chose carefully. History records that men wept over not being selected. They understood it was a history-changing opportunity and an honor. The entire country tracked their progress as newspapers got occasional updates. They were regarded as heroes.

I believe with all my heart that to walk with God in the wilderness of this fallen world is the noblest thing any man or woman can do. To walk with God and engage Him in every realm of life—while in budget meetings, making sales calls, reading bedtime stories, watching television, doing laundry, and having dinner with family or friends—is more valued by God than we can possibly know. And choosing Him in daily moments fundamentally affects others for generations to come.

If you are a follower of Jesus, you already know that the rest of the world sees you as at least a little crazy. But if you are thinking of getting more serious about walking with Him, you need to know that you may face opposition even from friends or family. This may range from those who think you are simply misguided to those who find your relationship with Jesus offensive because of what it exposes in them.

But no matter what others believe, waking up every morning knowing that God planned every part of your day and wants to experience it with you is the greatest adventure you could have. What will He say to you? How will He use you in the lives of others? What aspect of His heart or hand will you see today? How will He use your circumstances for good? What unseen enemies, difficulties, and hardships will you confront together? What moments of great joy and prosperity will you celebrate?

The stakes are high. The consequences of how we live will have an impact on history. There is absolutely nothing better you can do for your family, your friends, or your coworkers than to walk closely with God. And God will be extravagant throughout all eternity in the rewards He gives His children for doing so.

Walking with Jesus is not easy. I have friends who think spiritual progress will happen without effort. They envision life as a cruise where Jesus is the Captain and their job is to enjoy the ride and some good fellowship along the way as they avoid moral failure. But that's not what walking with God is like. When our view of walking with God is that small and trivial, we can waste our lives even as Christians. We can miss most of what God wants to give us and remain bystanders while others have adventures with God. It fills me with fear and deep sadness that this may describe the majority of the Western church today. We were born to live the highest existence on earth. We are called to far more than the ordinary life that many settle for.

Walking with God isn't just about reading the Bible, not doing bad things, and going to church. It is much simpler and much harder than that. I've experienced two main steps to take toward the Father that are as complementary as two feet walking. The first is *seeing* God clearly and the second is *responding* to Him accordingly. Think of it as the rhythm of the right and left foot moving together, each contributing to progress and each essential for forward motion. This is how spiritual progress happens. The more you see God, the more you respond to Him. The more you respond to Him, the more you see Him clearly and the more of Him you experience. Your companionship with Jesus deepens, and you increasingly recognize your life to be the privileged existence it is, no matter your circumstances. The rest of the book will unpack these ideas. The rest of my life—and I hope yours—will be about learning to *live* them!

WORTH THE SACRIFICE

The Lewis and Clark team committed its share of mistakes, missteps, and general clumsiness on their journey because they failed to follow their guide. It has been the same for me in my walk with God. How many times have I done my own thing because I doubted God's intention to give me His best? How many decisions have I made without seeking His counsel? How many times could I have traded up and instead traded down? I'm discouraged at times by how foolish I can be. But until heaven, the goal is not perfection. We must not put that standard on ourselves or imagine that God does. We're all still growing up. We make mistakes daily. But God does not get disgusted with us. I did not expect my kids to act like forty-year-olds when they were two; I had patience with them, knowing they weren't very far along on the journey. God has patience with us too. He knows we won't be perfect until we finish the journey and start eternity with Him.

Walking with God is the hardest thing you will ever do. I am sorry if someone told you otherwise. Life this side of heaven will test your love and loyalty to God. It will test your determination and your confidence in His leadership. You will have to face regular revelations of how sinful you really are behind the facade. I know from experience that there will be hardship, discouragement, and difficulty you cannot imagine. There's no question about whether it is worth it, but understand that walking with Him will cost you dearly.

On the other hand, when you walk with God you avoid a lot of self-inflicted pain that people suffer when they go their own way. And life is much more pleasant if you can live above your circumstances, instead of under their awful weight, by relying on His strength and power. Life is much simpler when only *one thing* really matters to you.

You will have seasons of not surrendering to His will. You will also have seasons of accelerated growth. You will fail to seek God's direction. Personally, I have never had a day of continual engagement with God every moment of the day no matter how hard I've tried. But I am learning to accept that every day is a new day with the Lord. You have to move on from mistakes and keep looking forward. Ask Him to forgive you, and then forgive yourself as He has forgiven you.

>>   The good news is that the single most impor-
      tant step we will ever take with God is the
      next one. >>

The main objective is to keep walking every day, making steady if not quick progress. Traveling the same path as Lewis and Clark made it clear to me that the explorers had days in which the best they could hope for was incremental progress— one foot in front of the other. Speed was not the most important thing; it was making it to the finish line—enduring to the end. The same is true for those of us who walk with God.

The good news is that the single most important step we will ever take with God is the next one. We can only take one step at a time. God knows this; He made us this way. And He is so gracious with each of us. He honors even the simplest sincere efforts to walk with Him. He exaggerates the good things we do and does not discipline us for every foolish decision we make. He doesn't ask us to obey every principle and every command at once. He doesn't demand that we learn all the lessons from all of Scripture in a single moment. But our Father does ask us to be intentional about walking with Him one step at a time. That's how it works. By one decision, one attitude, one response, one thought at a time, we walk toward home.

C. S. Lewis's greatest passion was helping people find their deepest satisfaction in God. He knew that a fuller understanding of God's character changes the way we think about life with Him. Here is what he wrote in *The Weight of Glory*:

> If there lurks in most modern minds the notion that to desire our own good and earnestly to hope for the enjoyment of it is a bad thing, I submit that this notion has crept in from Kant and the Stoics and is no part of the Christian faith. Indeed, if we consider the unblushing promises of reward and the staggering nature of the rewards promised in the Gospels, it would seem that Our Lord finds our desires not too strong, but too weak. We are half-hearted creatures, fooling about with drink and sex and ambition when infinite joy is offered us, like an ignorant child who wants to go on making mud pies in a slum because he cannot imagine what is meant by the offer of a holiday at the sea. We are far too easily pleased.[1]

I don't want to be "far too easily pleased." I want a stronger desire for all the joy, pleasure, and adventure that is to be found in walking with God this side of heaven. I want to eagerly obey the command and receive the promise of Psalm 37:4: *"Delight yourself in the LORD; and He will give you the desires of your heart."*

ENCOUNTERING GOD SUGGESTION

Consider this: If in every circumstance you face today, you were convinced that every good response to God was *vastly* better than being indifferent or independent, how would that change the frequency and quality of your response to Him? Today, pause just a few moments and remind yourself of His devotion to give you His best and of His unchanging loyalty. See if that gives you a different outlook on your day.

CHAPTER FOUR

MOMENTUM

Encountering the Source

I was on a business trip to Florida a few years after the season of renewal that began in 2002. On the last day of the trip, I woke early and enjoyed some incredible interaction with the Holy Spirit while I read my Bible. It was as if when I awoke, the world had been a black-and-white screen, and then during my time with Him, it became full, high-definition color. More than just physically awake, I was now awake to an amazing God and feeling excited about what lay in store that day. Afterward, I asked for wisdom for situations I knew I would face, for favor with an executive who was upset with our firm, for insight to help a client, and for God's power to see and respond to Him throughout the day.

As the day progressed, Jesus and I quietly interacted before, during, and after my meetings. He actively drew me into fellowship with Him and even whispered thoughts to me throughout the day. I would ask for wisdom, and the next words out of my mouth would be exactly the solution we needed. At one point I asked Him if I should join in a particular conversation and felt prompted to keep quiet. Later, it was obvious that my silence kept me from saying the wrong thing. I spiritually multitasked all day: paying attention to the people, projects, and conversations in the meetings I was in and, at the same time, looking past them to see God in complete control of everything.

Whenever Jesus spoke to me, answered a prayer, or opened my eyes to see Him with me that day, I responded with simple thanks. There is something wonderful and right about telling God how much I admire and appreciate Him. He certainly does not *need* a compliment from me, but I benefit from verbalizing how grateful and amazed I am.

I remember thinking, *Why don't I pursue more of these rich experiences with Him?* Approaching the day as an adventure with God gave me a kind of childlike optimism, like watching a drama on television knowing the hero has to survive so the series can continue. I knew that even difficulties would eventually turn out for good.

And there *were* difficulties. In one especially challenging meeting, an executive seemed unfairly upset and I was tempted to respond defensively. But knowing that my heavenly Father was with me and in full control altered my response. I could thank Him for the solution He was about to bring even if the solution was to help me respond well to injustice instead of delivering the outcome for which I'd prayed. God gave me plenty of grace for that meeting.

At the end of the day, I caught a cab to the airport. When the Holy Spirit prompted me to talk to the driver about Jesus, I was a little annoyed. I was tired and wanted a mental and emotional break. But reluctantly I began the dialogue God was leading me to have.

As the driver and I talked, I learned that he had been thinking lately about God's place in his life. It dawned on me that I was there for a noble purpose: to tell a stranger about how amazing Jesus has been for me and how he could experience the same life. Our discussion was timely, and I got out of the car feeling exuberant. "Thank You for not letting me resist You, Lord," I told God. I was reminded again how His plans and agenda are always monumentally better than mine.

Waiting in line at the airport, I prayed for a good seat assignment with plenty of elbow room. I even used the self-serving argument that the right seat would allow me to read the Bible and write in my journal more easily. When I reached the counter, I got the best seat possible and was immediately embarrassed at God's goodness in the face of my attempt to finesse Him.

A PERFECT DAY

After my flight took off, I reflected on the incredible day I'd just had. I mentally recounted every time God helped me with a project, provided an answer to a tough question, or gave me favor with someone. Ten to twelve such incidents came easily to mind from this day full of God stories. I sensed a little of the vast, unseen world where God towers above everything.

I opened my Bible and used a psalm as the context for admiring Him. Awe, contentment, and joy filled me as I reflected on His infinite power, love, and wisdom. When I focused on my sovereign and supreme Ruler, my business worries melted like wax. I sensed that everything would be okay—not easy and not always fair, but okay. I knew I would have everything that really mattered. What an unspeakable, undeserved honor and privilege to have a relationship with such a God!

>> I decided that whatever a "perfect" day with Jesus was, I wanted to devote the rest of my life to pursuing it. >>

A tap on my shoulder interrupted my interaction with God. I looked up to see a flight attendant about my daughter's age. She asked, "Do you have any idea how happy you look? I've been standing in the front of the plane watching your face for a while. You seem so full of joy!" Without giving me a chance to reply, she turned and walked back to her station at the front of the plane.

I was stunned. I had been so focused on God that I wasn't aware of what was going on around me. Then I recalled a quote that had stood out to me when I read it some time before. Frank Laubach wrote in *Letters by a Modern Mystic*,

Any hour of any day may be made perfect by merely choosing. It is perfect if one looks toward God that entire hour, waiting for His leadership . . . and trying hard to do every tiny thing exactly as God wishes it done. . . . The most important discovery of my whole life is that one can take a little rough cabin and transform it into a palace by flooding it with God.

"Any hour of any day may be made perfect." What a comment! I decided that whatever a "perfect" day with Jesus was, I wanted to devote the rest of my life to pursuing it. I knew I would never

be perfect here on earth and would likely never have a truly perfect day before eternity, but I wanted the *full-strength* version of paradise—as much as God would give me this side of heaven.

The word that came to mind was *momentum*. As I described in chapter 2, I had lost momentum in enjoying God in 2002. I had settled for an academic and nominal engagement with Him. But I had tasted a richer and more life-giving way of walking with God, and I wanted more of it. I wanted the desire for God to be the controlling passion of my life. I knew no light switch existed that could ignite that desire, only the steady and determined effort to renew my commitment to progress every day of my life. I longed to end this cycle in which I had days filled with amazing experiences with Him, followed by other days that fell utterly flat. I wanted momentum from one day to the next day to the day after that.

AN HONORED GUEST

I turned my attention to the Gospels. How did Jesus talk about life with God? What did He say it should look like? I wanted something concrete that would show me how to gain momentum in knowing and following Jesus.

I found great insight in Jesus' message to His disciples the night before He was murdered. In His last minutes with them, Jesus patiently explained what their companionship with Him would be like after He returned to heaven.

The disciples' grief and confusion about what was happening clouded their ability to understand Jesus' words. The incredible adventure of the last three years seemed to be coming to an unexpected and abrupt end. The most winsome Person who ever lived had been their teacher and friend and had cared for them as no one else ever had. Now Jesus was telling them that after He left and went to heaven they would enjoy an even closer relationship with Him because God's empowering Holy Spirit would be in them. He told them, *"But I tell you the truth, it is to your advantage that I go away; for if I do not go away, the Helper will not come to you; but if I go, I will send Him to you"* (John 16:7).

Earlier in the same conversation, Jesus had given the disciples a word picture to describe this new relationship. With royal authority, He issued a command and a stunning promise. The command was to abide in Jesus. The incredible promise was that He will reciprocate by abiding in us (see John 15:4).

The word *abide* was full of rich meaning in the ancient Middle Eastern context in which Jesus lived. If a stranger needed shelter, he would be invited to live in a person's home with his family. The host would do everything possible to make him feel welcomed and honored. He'd include him at every meal and give him the best food. He'd invite him to be a part of every conversation and to join in every activity. Life would be done together.

>> If you are ever confused about how to relate to God in any moment, just ask yourself, If I really believed Jesus was right next to me, how would I treat Him? >>

My son Jason and his wife, Katie, were missionaries in a Middle Eastern country for four years. Jason had the chance to go into the desert where Bedouin nomads live today as their ancestors did thousands of years ago, in tents shared with animals and living off the land. Though a stranger, he was received as royalty. He was invited to stay with them as long as he liked. He was given the best of their food. He enjoyed hours of conversation with his hosts through his interpreter. All activity of the family centered around him because he was their guest. They bent over backward to see that he felt welcomed and honored. In their culture, to do otherwise would be unthinkably rude.

This is the imagery Jesus called to mind with His followers when He used the word *abide.* He was issuing to us a call to welcome Him into our lives with the same attention, respect, and desire to please and know Him that my son received in a Bedouin tent.

If you are ever confused about how to relate to God in any moment, just ask yourself, *If I really believed Jesus was right next to me, how would I treat Him? If He were to come to my home and stay with me, how would I incorporate Him into my life?* Abiding in Christ is simply relating to Him much as we would any other person. It is being thoughtful of what would please Him and sensitive to His desires. It means we set aside focusing only on ourselves to focus on our royal Guest. And it requires an extra measure of attentiveness because this Guest is, after all, unseen. But unlike with some guests in your home, you will find great life and joy in this relationship. Jesus is never a burden. He reciprocates with greater kindness, friendliness, and generosity than any other guest could possibly offer.

Abiding is the New Testament picture of paradise. It is the fulfillment of David's bold declaration,

> *I have set the LORD continually before me; because He is at my right hand, I will not be shaken. Therefore my heart is glad and my glory rejoices; my flesh also will dwell securely.*

You will make known to me the path of life; in Your presence is fullness of joy; in Your right hand there are pleasures forever. (Psalm 16:8-9,11)

On my near-perfect day in Florida, I had another taste of the paradise David described: living with a sense of God continually before me, being consciously aware of Him and attentive to His desires, enjoying fellowship and the great adventure of following Him, remaining unshaken by challenges, experiencing fullness of joy and gratitude. The more moments we connect with Him in this way, the more momentum we build toward constant abiding.

A VITAL CONNECTION

When Jesus introduced the concept of abiding, He used an analogy of a branch connected to the trunk: *"I am the vine, you are the branches; he who abides in Me and I in him, he bears much fruit, for apart from Me you can do nothing"* (John 15:5).

Jesus' disciples knew exactly what He meant by this agricultural metaphor. They knew that the vine is the source of all the life-giving nutrition and vitality for the branches. In this verse Jesus passionately calls out to us that He *alone* is the source of life. He is the only source of lasting joy, companionship, satisfaction, and everything else the human heart craves.

We all look *somewhere* for our source of life. Many of my friends and I are tempted to find our source of life in career achievement, money, or status. Others find it in children, friends, hobbies, and recreation. We can easily identify what is most important to us by what we dream about, pray about, worry about, and long for in our free moments. It's the thing that gives us our sense of worth.

It's the last priority we let go of when time squeezes us. But the Son of God speaks clearly: The life we were created to enjoy can be found only in Him; He must become our controlling passion. There is only one place to find paradise. Everything else is a mirage.

To abide in Jesus like a branch abiding with its vine means that every day we draw our life from Him instead of things in the seen world. While we are going to work, raising a family, and enjoying friends, He urges us to remain focused on a bigger world and a very present Source of life. When we grab on to the fullness of what this means, everything becomes much clearer. We are not the vine. Our spouse or best friend isn't the vine. Our kids aren't the vine. Our stuff isn't the vine. *Jesus is the Vine.* Our life comes from knowing and following Him. The more of this life we experience, the more heaven comes to earth for us and others.

The connection of a branch to a vine is not occasional; it is continual. Likewise, the experience Jesus calls us to is one of continually seeking Him throughout each day. Ideally, in every moment we would be connected to Him and drawing our life from Him. That would be a perfect day.

Our lives are a series of moments in the presence of God. Abiding is engaging God in these moments by treating Him as our royal Guest. The more moments we connect with God in this way, the more paradise we will experience. The more we abide, the more the life-giving force flows from the Vine (Jesus) to the branches (us).

The opposite of abiding is living out our moments unaware of God's presence and indifferent to what pleases Him. It is being so self-absorbed that we don't even think of God and so self-willed that we do only what we want without considering what He wants. We choose self-reliance over trusting His counsel, His character, and His wisdom.

We are free to live this way. Yet a self-focused life is the most empty, shallow, and nominal life on the planet. Here is how Jesus described it: *"If anyone does not abide in Me, he is thrown away as a branch and dries up; and they gather them, and cast them into the fire and they are burned"* (John 15:6). This is stunning imagery. A branch disconnected from the Source will be lifeless, unable to fulfill its purpose. This is how I felt in December 2002. And I still feel this way today when I have a day with little or no interaction with Jesus. I come home dry and empty, as if I am missing something vital. If you have ever experienced the life-giving force of abiding in Christ, you know how dissatisfying it is to live independent of Him.

MULTITASKING

I was sharing this material with a group of men when one got pretty frustrated with me. His life, he insisted, was so filled with work and family responsibilities that he was too busy to connect with God like this. He claimed he would have to give up his job and become a monk!

I understood his response, and I told him so. I agreed that thinking of God and responding to Him in the midst of a busy day takes concentration and effort. But I also explained that I believe living this way is possible; were it not, Jesus would not have commanded it of us. He wouldn't dangle paradise in front of us and then give us an impossible path to find it.

The fact is, in our modern world we multitask all the time. We text, e-mail, and take calls amid all kinds of activity. All we have to do to engage God is turn our thoughts to Him in the flash of a moment—on an elevator, waiting in line, while on hold—anytime and anywhere. Could it be that busyness isn't the real issue?

For me, the problem is never that I am too busy to enjoy God, only that I am too self-absorbed. Or sometimes I have such a low view of God in that moment that I find it a burden, not a great privilege, to engage Him. I get tense, stressed, or frustrated—completely focused on *my* challenges, *my* problems, and how *I* feel—leaving little room for thoughts of Him. Even though I am utterly convinced that my best moments on the earth have occurred on days such as the one I described at the start of this chapter, I still live for hours with little or no real connection to God. Then eventually I wake up as though from a sleep and reengage Him. And He is always eager for us to reconnect. This is what life with God is like this side of heaven.

>> For me, the problem is never that I am too busy to enjoy God, only that I am too self-absorbed. Or sometimes I have such a low view of God in that moment that I find it a burden, not a great privilege, to engage Him. >>

It is a curious thing to pursue a goal we will never fully obtain in our lifetime. And if the goal is unreachable, why not give up? Why not just go for something easier? Because it is so much better to make progress toward a high and noble goal, the only one that will bring true life, than to pursue goals that will never satisfy. Better to make some progress in the right direction—toward an amazing God—than to give up and go in the wrong direction.

It is very much like an Olympic athlete preparing for the race of his or her life with serious intent, deliberate focus, and daily concentration. All else in life is a lower priority than the pleasure found in a goal that will bring honor. The athlete never experiences a *perfect* run; there are just *daily* runs, some slower than others, but all with the goal in sight. Progress is slow, hard fought, and uneven, but it is worth it. How much more is this true for the follower of Jesus!

Paul made a statement that stirs my heart and reinvigorates my resolve to make progress:

> *Not that I have already obtained it or have already become perfect, but I press on so that I may lay hold of that for which also I was laid hold of by Christ Jesus. . . . I do not regard myself as having laid hold of it yet; but one thing I do: forgetting what lies behind and reaching forward to what lies ahead, I press on toward the goal for the prize of the upward call of God in Christ Jesus.* (Philippians 3:12-14)

The true follower of Jesus has one all-important goal in sight: finding all the pleasure, adventure, nobility, and relational connection with God as is possible. Even when we fall short, we have great confidence that we are pursuing what's best. At first, we may attain our goal only a few times a day when we manage to turn our thoughts to Jesus. But over time we will learn to fight for more moments in which we relate to Him as our honored Guest. That momentum is one of the major signs of spiritual maturity.

THE FORK IN THE ROAD

We've seen that in any moment, in any setting, we face a fork in the road: to respond to our royal Guest by connecting with Him or not to respond in this way. To abide or not to abide. Because God is always present, we respond to Him in one way or the other at any given time; there is no neutral ground.

Sadly, many religious people miss this significant truth. They are duped into thinking that if they are familiar with the truths of the Bible and avoid major sin, they are living life with God. In the book of Revelation, Jesus challenged this deception in a church in the town of Laodicea. These churchgoers were missing the point. They were proud of their faith and good theology and righteous activities, but they did not honor Jesus as their Guest. They rudely excluded Him from their daily activities, growing more and more independent of Him over time. In their indifference, they didn't even notice His absence when He left. They thought of themselves as rich in their relationship with God when they were actually poor! They pretended to be connected to God but were really connected to a false vine, perhaps the vine of wealth and comfort. This is the essence of the religious attitude Jesus corrected in His ministry—pretending to connect with God but still living life on our terms.

Jesus invited them to acknowledge the truth.

> *Because you say, "I am rich, and have become wealthy, and have need of nothing," and you do not know that you are wretched and miserable and poor and blind and naked, I advise you to buy from Me gold refined by fire so that you may become rich, and white garments so that you may clothe yourself, and that the shame of your nakedness will not be revealed; and eye salve to anoint your eyes so that you may see. Those whom I love, I reprove and discipline; therefore be zealous and repent.* (Revelation 3:17-19)

What comes next speaks volumes of how passionately God wants to abide with His children. Rather than condemning or dismissing them, Jesus urged them to let Him into their thoughts and affections again. Even as He corrected their deception, He invited them to return to abiding with Him. He wanted to live among them. Jesus went on to say, *"Behold, I stand at the door and knock; if anyone hears My voice and opens the door, I will come in to him and will dine with him, and he with Me"* (verse 20).

What a stunning image! The Son of God is portrayed outside their home, disconnected from how they live, but He is not angry, pouting, or even demanding. Instead, the most gracious Person who ever lived is simply knocking. Make sure you don't miss this! Even when we are indifferent to God for a while, He still welcomes our fellowship. He still knocks at our door. And He doesn't quit knocking. As a gentleman, He will not force Himself upon us, but He will never stop knocking until we open the door. We'll talk more about this in a later chapter, but I hope you will hold this image in your mind and heart.

How will we respond to such a God? Will we welcome Him into everything we are doing? Will we let Him lead us in what to say or do? Will we interact with Him? Will we find our joy in life by pursuing Him and experiencing more happiness in knowing Him than in anything else? Or will we live indifferent to His presence, as though He does not matter or is not there? That's our fork in the road. Life is not about the rules we keep or the Bible knowledge we gain but about how we respond to God in the situations we face every day.

The same God who patiently pursues us promises to provide the inner strength we need to live in moment-by-moment connection with Him. We are not on our own. In fact, when we are walking with God, He does most of the work.

When my son Jason was three years old, I let him sit in my lap while I drove a tractor. He put his hands on the wheel, and I gave him instructions on how to steer. I directed the machine, I anticipated what to do next, and I knew what the yard should ultimately look like when the work was completed. There is a parallel in our life with God. God does 99 percent of the work, and we're responsible for the remainder. It is never all up to us! God gives us all the help we need to walk with Him, to abide with Him, and to be led by His Spirit rather than by our flesh.

MOMENTUM IN THE RIGHT DIRECTION

If I could speak to you as a father, I would tell you that you will have good days and bad days of inviting God into your daily life. You will make a ton of mistakes along the way. No one but Jesus has ever had a perfect day with our heavenly Father. *But the most important thing in your soul is the desire for more moments of engaging our amazing God*—the desire to approach each day with a clean slate and walk with our great King through the wilderness of your daily life. The desire for more pleasure in Him, more adventure, more experiences of living above your circumstances, and more revelations of the hand and heart of God in every day. Cultivating a fire, a thirst, a hunger for God is the most important thing you can do.

>> The most important thing in your soul is the desire for more moments of engaging our amazing God. >>

On the other hand, the *worst* condition of your heart is to be complacent, to settle, to subtly shift your ambition to something besides Jesus. This is status quo for many Christians; they may have started well, but few finish well. Most slowly, with each passing decade, begin to find their source in something or someone other than Jesus. Many are led by toxic selfishness even if they hide it well.

Your life has momentum in one of two directions. You are either inviting God into your thoughts, affections, decisions, and conversations more today than last month—or you're doing this less. You're either experiencing more of paradise this month than you were last month—or less. It is not as if you just "get it" one day and your path is set for life. Momentum requires a daily— even hourly—recommitment to a path.

Please don't underestimate the value of slow progress. Even a few more moments a day of seeing and responding to Him can make a fundamental change in your life. Remember, every day brims with new opportunity. Jesus told us not to worry about tomorrow, for there is so much opportunity to seek Him today that it should occupy all our energy (see Matthew 6:33-34).

The rest of this book is designed to help you in the cardinal ways we enjoy God and respond to Him as our Guest and Guide on our life journey. My earnest hope is to help you obtain momentum in your walk with God. I promise to give you the best of what I have imperfectly learned and relearned and experienced. I am only a fellow traveler with you. But I will not settle, and I hope you won't either. I want more for me and for you.

Chapter 5 is about seeing God clearly because that is where our motivation to walk with God begins. Chapters 6 through 10 are about how we engage Him and find life in Him daily, whatever our circumstances or experiences. Some topics, such as conversing with or trusting God, will sound familiar at first. But when viewed from the foundation of these first four chapters, I believe they will take on new depth and wonder for you as they have for me.

What you're about to learn is only the beginning. It is in the practice—the actual living out—of these truths that you will enjoy God and the great adventure of life with Him. You'll never master any of them, but the more progress you make in responding to God, the more paradise you will enjoy. That's a goal worthy of our greatest passion.

ENCOUNTERING GOD SUGGESTIONS

How would you describe your spiritual momentum today? Are you enjoying more or fewer moments with Him this month than last? Ask God what would have to change in order for you to have positive momentum and then be quiet for a moment and see what He brings to mind.

Before you start one or two activities today—a drive to work, a project, a conversation—mentally invite Jesus into the activity, thank Him that He is there, and welcome Him to interact with you.

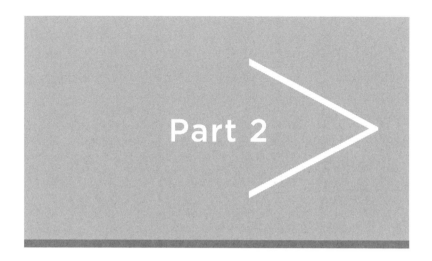

Part 2

ENJOYING
GOD

CHAPTER FIVE

SEEING GOD CLEARLY

Responding to God's majesty

I thought I knew how captivating and majestic mountains could be. After all, I attended the U.S. Air Force Academy, which is situated at the base of a beautiful mountain in the Colorado Rockies. Incredible mountain views greeted me as I walked to class, played sports, or glanced out the window of my room. In my free time, my favorite thing to do was to go hiking. After graduation, I experienced the quiet grandeur of West Virginia's mountains and the stark beauty of those in New Mexico. Later, on business travel, I visited the picturesque Swiss Alps. The sight of mountains gives me perspective on what is important in life in a way I cannot fully describe. I prefer mountains to any other scenery on earth.

In 2006, I was able to take my boys with me on a speaking engagement in Anchorage. Our hosts gave us the gift of a week at a wilderness camp deep in the heart of Alaska. I discovered that the mountains of Alaska are different from any I'd seen before. My previous concept of the size, scope, and beauty of a typical mountain paled in comparison.

Early in the morning, on the first day of our trip, our skilled guide, Paul Klaus, flew Jason and me in a small aircraft to the base of one of the largest and most remote mountains in the world: Mount Saint Elias. (Sadly, my son Matt wasn't feeling well that day and couldn't join us for this excursion.) I find it impossible to describe adequately how massive Mount Saint Elias is. Starting at sea level and soaring to eighteen thousand feet, it makes the Rockies look like the Texas hill country.

Wrapping around the base in the mountain's foreground was a gigantic twenty-story glacier. A small bay lay between the glacier and us. As we watched, five-story chunks of the blue ice cracked and fell off into the ocean with a sound as loud as thunder. It took our breath away. Standing arm in arm, Jason and I just stared, wordless with awe. It was cold but we hardly noticed. The mountain arrested all our attention. We felt privileged knowing that few will ever get to this remote place hundreds of miles from the nearest road.

Then things got even better. We took off from our landing strip and soared to an altitude that allowed us to see the peak of the mountain up close. As we turned north past Mount Saint Elias, we were shocked to see a vast ocean of massive mountains that stretched for hundreds of miles in all directions with glaciers weaving around their bases. A lifetime wouldn't be enough to explore them all, but the one I'd just seen made me want to move my family to a small cabin nearby and try. We were so captivated by the beauty and grandeur around us that the stress and problems of the rest of our lives lost importance. A mixture of peace, happiness, and true joy mingled with a hunger for more. This was much more than a pleasant vacation outing. It changed our lives in a way that made us want to sacrifice time, money, and energy to have more of it.

I noticed something else. It wasn't enough to talk to each other about the incredible things we'd seen; we couldn't wait to share our pictures and stories with Matt and the rest of our family and friends. We told everyone we knew, "You *have* to see Mount Saint Elias!" I have never gotten over it and don't expect I ever will.

MADE TO SAVOR MAJESTY

Majesty transforms us. It elevates our vision and heightens our desire for more. Magnificent scenery like mountains, waterfalls, canyons, and forests fills us with joy and an oddly wonderful sense of smallness. It reminds us of what really matters. When we see majesty, we're moved to tell others about it and invite them to enjoy it too. Most important of all, the majesty of nature points to the majesty of the Creator, who made all of it for us to enjoy. The contours of God's greatness and majesty are infinitely more transforming than a rock in Alaska.

God is a Person, and, like any person, He has attributes of character and personality. We share some of these, such as love, affection, friendliness, and compassion but to a far lesser degree than they are displayed in God. Other attributes of God are His alone, such as the ability to be present everywhere in the universe and the fact that He has no beginning or end.

After our trip to Alaska, it dawned on me one day that knowing God is like exploring the mountain range we saw there. Everything about Him is majestic and transforming, and He has an ocean of attributes to explore.

I could try to plumb the depths of God's wisdom, for example, for the rest of eternity and never learn all that God knows. I can meditate on Scripture or ponder the wisdom that created the universe, and it elevates my desire to know God better and trust Him more. But even such lofty thoughts barely scratch the surface of every wise act, plan, motive, and thought of God.

I have a similar experience when I reflect on God's power. I don't know how He maintains the orbit of every planet, is able to hold all the oceans in the palms of His hands, and causes each flower to bloom. His power to create the universe and then sustain every molecule in it leaves me in awe. His ability to change the human heart to become more like Jesus' heart overwhelms me.

Many more attributes beg to be explored, each with the power to captivate and transform us. I haven't even touched on the kindness, compassion, affection, loyalty, goodness, and sovereignty of God. We were created to be captivated with His majesty and arrested by His greatness. We exist to see and savor the greatness of God and find our greatest joy in knowing Him.

No wonder David made this extraordinary statement: *"One thing I have asked from the LORD, that I shall seek: That I may dwell in the house of the LORD all the days of my life, to behold the beauty of the LORD and to meditate in His temple"* (Psalm 27:4). It may seem a stretch at first to agree with David that of all the things we could ask for from God, the most important is the honor and pleasure of exploring His nature every day of our lives. But the best thing He could do for us is reveal more of Himself. And His determined intention is to arrest our attention and affection with His majesty. In fact, it is His passion.

GOD'S RELENTLESS PASSION

God is relentless in revealing His greatness and goodness to us throughout every day. Like everything God cares about, this is no passing interest or casual desire. He is always actively and deliberately shining a light on the depth of His power, love, kindness, beauty, and more. As Jonathan Edwards said with elegance, "God looks on the communication of himself and the emanation of his glory to belong to the fulness and completeness of himself."[1] Said another way, God is infinitely passionate about revealing fresh glimpses of His greatness and goodness to us every day. It is His nature to do so, and He loves giving us the most life-giving and life-changing gift possible. An Old Testament prophet said it this way: *"For the earth will be filled with the knowledge of the glory of the LORD, as the waters cover the sea"* (Habakkuk 2:14). We cannot grasp this side of heaven how actively God is revealing His nature to us. He desperately wants us to pay attention so that we won't miss the discovery.

>> God is relentless in revealing His greatness and goodness to us throughout every day. >>

God constantly reveals His *heart* and His *hand*. When I say He reveals His heart, I'm referring to how He feels when He looks at us, what He is passionate about, what He hates, and what makes Him laugh. It includes His motives and what He values.

God reveals His hand to us in how He provides for, protects, and sustains us every day in the details of life. He uses our circumstances as a theater for displaying His power, wisdom, grace, and good intentions toward us. A proper view of our lives will cause us to stand in speechless awe at a God this good, this powerful, and this majestic.

The older I get the more I'm convinced that God's revelation of who He is turns out to be His greatest gift to us. It is the kindest and most generous thing He could do for us. I am also convinced from my experience and from the Scriptures that the most joyful people on earth are those who enjoy a mental image of God's greatness that expands over the course of their lives. They are God-enthralled; they see Him in the Scriptures, in their lives, and in creation. They recognize that He is always present, loyal, and active. As a result they live above their circumstances. They are filled with gratitude for all the good gifts He has given them rather than complaining about what they don't have. They naturally draw others to find joy in God as they do. And they discover more of His majesty daily.

PERCEPTION IS CRUCIAL

What we perceive about the nature of God determines how we respond to Him throughout each day. The respected twentieth-century pastor and teacher A. W. Tozer wrote in *The Knowledge of the Holy*,

> What comes to mind when we think about God, is the most important thing about us. . . . We tend by a secret

law of the soul to move toward our mental image of God. . . . Were we to extract from any man a complete answer to the question, "What comes to mind when you think about God?" we might predict with absolute certainty the spiritual future of that man.[2]

In other words, how you answer the question "Who is God *to you?*" is the single most determinative factor in your spiritual direction.

Tozer wasn't talking about what we'd say to friends from our Bible study or reading group, or whether we agree with the doctrine of our church. What matters more are our inner conclusions about God in a given moment. Whether or not we are aware of it, we are continually determining how relevant God is to our situation. Right or wrong, we all decide at numerous points during each day what we believe about how Jesus views what we think, feel, and say. We decide whether His leadership is better than ours. We also decide whether He is the greatest Source of joy or whether we should look to our own goals and agenda.

The strongest determiner of how much paradise we experience on earth is how we perceive God. All motivation to correctly respond to Him springs from an accurate perception.

If, while I am on my way to work, I reflect on God's deep interest in every part of my day and His passion for fellowship with me, then I will *want* to talk to Him and hear Him speak to me. On the other hand, if I assume He is small, irrelevant, or disinterested in me, I will drive to work alone in my thoughts and remain indifferent to Him.

If I perceive that God has my best interests in mind and is infinitely powerful and wise, I will *want* to follow His leadership.

If, however, I perceive Him as capricious or cruel, then I will navigate life as though He does not exist. It all pivots on my perception of God *in that moment*. Because my perception of Him is so fluid, I need to constantly feed my mind with truth and replace the lies and limitations I place on Him.

To journey through life with an ever-expanding view of God, shaped by careful and deliberate discovery of the truth about Him, is the greatest triumph on earth. Fear, stress, anger, depression, pain, difficulty, worthlessness, and shame all melt in light of the truth of who He is and how passionate He is to father us. At the same time, to carry a low view of God is the worst tragedy a Christ-follower could suffer. To hardly think of Him or to have low thoughts of Him will ruin your life, your relationships, and the legacy God wants to give you even if you are a nice person, go to church regularly, and are basically moral by human standards. Every spiritual problem we have is sourced in a distorted view of God.

Looking back over the last four decades, I believe we who have been teachers and leaders in the church have largely failed to teach what God is really like. We have overemphasized living a godly lifestyle to the near exclusion of knowing God personally. Most Christians leave a church service or small-group meeting thinking they ought to be better people when in fact they should leave captivated by what an amazing God we have. When this happens week after week, we miss the point that paradise is not about being better boys and girls but about being enthralled with knowing and following God.

Perceiving the truth about God is what life is all about; miss this and you miss everything. To choose to explore God and know Him, thinking of Him correctly with an ever-expanding view, will ensure your life ends in great triumph!

SEEING GOD CHANGES US

I hope you've seen that discovering the depth and breadth of God's character will captivate you, thrill you, and draw you into an amazing life with Him. Yet God has even more in mind for you. His clear aim is also to create a fundamental shift in your heart and mind.

His goal is to take a self-centered person like me and transform my heart and mind until I love to please God more than myself. He wants to change my heart from being self-reliant to trusting utterly in Him in every circumstance and becoming ever more confident in His character. He is in the business of taking self-absorbed people and captivating them with His majesty.

The catalyst for this remarkable change is His Spirit, who helps us see God and then respond to Him accordingly. You will recall from chapter 3 that this is the right foot and left foot of walking with God. We see Him (right foot) and then we respond to Him (left foot), causing us to see Him more clearly. It is a continuous cycle.

>> A fresh glimpse of God's greatness is the only lasting and effective motivator for knowing and following Him over a lifetime. >>

One of the questions I'm asked most often when I speak to groups is, "What can I do to restore or to ignite my passion for God?" I've seen only one thing change the human heart (mine or anyone else's): a fresh glimpse of God's greatness. This is the only lasting and effective motivator for knowing and following Him over a lifetime and is the transformational agent God provided to incline our hearts to respond to Him. We read of it in

2 Corinthians: *"But we all, with unveiled face, beholding as in a mirror the glory of the Lord, are being transformed into the same image from glory to glory, just as from the Lord, the Spirit"* (3:18).

Seeing God's glory has the power to change our orientation to Him, to our life circumstances, and even to ourselves. Just thinking about God reignites my interest in Him. Lingering for a few moments on an aspect of His nature brings life into proper focus. I always come away from gazing at God with greater clarity about my relationship with Him, my family, and the rest of the world.

Seeing His greatness gives us fearless courage in the face of life's challenges. We see what really matters, and the "little things"—such as whether we get a promotion or get into the school we want or live in the right house or apartment—lose importance. Glimpses of God's devotion and loyalty to us move us to want to follow Him and sacrifice for Him. When we get a proper view of God's delight in us, we want to delight in Him too. The more we admire Him, the more we want to imitate Him.

Life is full of challenges, and a bigger view of God is the only thing that will give us peace, confidence, and even optimism in every circumstance. In contrast, seeing God through a distorted lens that makes Him small, irrelevant, and less than competent will ruin our lives in many ways.

As in all of life with God, learning to see Him is a process, not a light switch. No one is enthralled with God completely on day one of the journey. Progress can be slow and hard fought, but that doesn't mean it isn't real. And God is always willing to provide generously all the help we need for that progress to occur. We must push through the fog of this world and our own self-focus to see Him clearly and savor His majesty every day. Stated simply, the single most important goal of life is to enjoy an ever-expanding mental image of God as we walk this earth and go about our business.

HOW TO SEE THE UNSEEN

Because God is invisible to our physical eyes as long as we're on earth, He has provided other ways for us to see Him. We've established already that seeing God has largely to do with how we perceive Him in our minds. We've also seen that it requires a deliberate choice on our part to turn away from apathy or an inward focus at any moment of the day and instead turn our thoughts toward Him to acknowledge His presence and reflect on His nature.

God assists us in this process by three primary means: He reveals Himself through the Bible, through His creation, and through life's circumstances. The road map to seeing the unseen God is pretty simple.

>> God reveals Himself through the Bible, through His creation, and through life's circumstances. >>

The Bible
The most important place we will discover the truth about God's character is in the Bible. Thousands of verses reveal who God is from many different angles. Each page reveals something about His capability, motives, integrity, loyalty, and brilliance. We can reflect on those truths, savor them, and allow the Holy Spirit to use them to expand our mental picture of God. Then we can respond by expressing our admiration.

Reading the Bible is not an academic exercise; it's a conversation. The Author is with you as you read, and you can ask Him what He wants to show you about Himself. Think of it as an interchange. You are constantly alert for what thought or truth is being unveiled—something completely new to you or a reminder of something wonderful that you have forgotten—and upon finding that truth, you talk with God about your discovery. On any given day, God may reveal a glimpse of His character that you have considered a hundred times before, but because of your life situation, He may reveal fresh implications or new dimensions. We can ask ourselves at the end of any day, What new insight into His character did He reveal to me today?

The Bible is also where we encounter Jesus, whose mission on earth was to reveal the true nature of God's character in all its beauty. To see the Son as revealed in the Scriptures is to see the Father, who *"in these last days has spoken to us in His Son, whom He appointed heir of all things, through whom also He made the world. And He is the radiance of His glory and the exact representation of His nature, and upholds all things by the word of His power"* (Hebrews 1:2-3).

Creation

Another way we can see God's character is to observe what He has made. Think about the elegance and intentionality of a cell that reveals God's power on a microscopic level. Watch a sunset and you'll see that He loves beauty. Notice how birds fly south for the winter in a formation that helps them stay together. In doing so, you are peering into a window of His greatness and wisdom. You can reflect on God's creativity and even His sense of humor when you notice what He has made for us to enjoy. All of creation is constantly telling us how great God is: *"The heavens are telling of the glory of God; and their expanse is declaring the work of His hands. Day to day pours forth speech, and night to night reveals knowledge"* (Psalm 19:1-2).

But we have to pay attention to see His work all around us. Part of the problem is that there is a world of difference between admiring a sunset and admiring the God who created it. I am amazed at how often I miss seeing Him in the gorgeous landscape we enjoy in Austin, Texas (or any other place I travel). All it takes to move beyond enjoying creation to interacting with the Creator is a conscious recognition that He exists and is the Artist who both imagined and crafted what we see.

Life's Circumstances

In addition to seeing God in the Bible and in His creation, we can see His hand in the events of life. Every event or circumstance is a new place for God to reveal His nature to those who are attentive. John Calvin, the sixteenth-century theologian, referred to daily life as a "dazzling theater" for God to reveal His greatness.[3]

When we are attentive to God in our circumstances, we'll start to perceive His hand when we receive favor at work. Whenever we have a good idea for how to solve a problem, how to do a project, or how to resolve a conflict, He is the author. Recently, my colleagues and I had trouble with a city official who was blocking one of our projects. No solution seemed possible. I had done everything I could think of. But when I asked God to help us, I was notified the next day that the official had changed his mind and, for the first time in city history, a policy was reversed without council approval. This was not due to my skill at negotiating. It was God's hand; He was showing me His love for me through His willingness to intervene on my behalf. I don't want to miss a single opportunity to see His hand in the circumstances of my life, thank Him for His help, and tell others how amazing He is.

Even in something as common as sitting down to a meal, we can glimpse the greatness of God. We have only to look past what is on our plates to see the hand of God in providing for our needs and managing His creation. He causes the rain to fall at the exact time needed for crops to grow. He planned, made, and sustains a complex ecosystem that each farm and field is a part of. He created people who made a global economy that sustains companies, and these companies employ people to pick and process foods, deliver it to grocery stores, and work the cash registers so we can purchase it. He provides jobs and abilities so we can earn money to buy the food. In this everyday provision, God reveals Himself to those who practice attentiveness toward Him.

Every good thing you have is a gift from the One who made you. Every good idea, every good impulse, every good circumstance, every act of love, every kindness on the earth is orchestrated by the One who is perfectly good and holy. Every time you see truth or beauty or goodness, it is God's way of calling us back to Himself and revealing His character. James rightly said, *"Every good thing given and every perfect gift is from above, coming down from the Father of lights, with whom there is no variation or shifting shadow"* (1:17).

REMOVING BLINDFOLDS

To be honest, I wake up every morning with a view of God that is unworthy of Him. I need continual reminders and fresh glimpses of what He has already revealed. I know it takes a deliberate and determined effort to see Him clearly, yet I struggle to make it a priority. That's because seeing God comes with a set of obstacles.

As I talked about in chapter 3, part of the reason for my struggle has to do with what happened when Adam and Eve sinned. When evil was introduced into the world, something inside us changed that makes it hard for us to see God clearly and accurately. Some call this our sinful, selfish, or old nature; others call it our flesh. By any name, it can blind us to the wonder of God's character.

Another reason we struggle to see God clearly is our Enemy, the Devil. The same liar who tempted Eve is still whispering lies about God in our minds. He works tirelessly to discredit God's character because he knows he can ruin our lives and often the lives of others if we have a wrong or incomplete view of God. Satan's goal is to dissuade us from following Jesus closely; he wants us to choose lives of indifference and independence instead. He will attempt to convince us that God is unfair, unwise, unkind, indifferent, or disgusted with us. He will insist that we are more competent in leading our lives than God is. He will tempt us to sit in judgment of God and find Him wanting. He will inflate in our minds our own wisdom. He will also try to shame us and make us feel inadequate to walk with God, as though only a few people have the innate skill to get close to Him and we are not among those few. We can always count on Him to use the main trick he used with Adam and Eve, the lie that God is giving us less than His best. To defeat this Enemy we can't see, we must consciously and continually reject lies and false notions about God and replace them with the truth of God's Word. This is why daily reminders and discoveries about God's character are essential. Rejecting lies and receiving the truth is a daily affair. If we are not vigilant, our view of God could contain more lies than truth.

Making progress against the gravity of our nature and the constant lies of the Enemy is like walking up a steep hill at times. The climb is most arduous during trials, which create yet another obstacle to seeing God clearly. I am most tempted to doubt His motives, wisdom, or power in seasons of difficulty.

It wasn't easy, for example, for Jan and me to see God's provision when our savings were lost and we had to start a new business just at the time we had hoped to retire. It wasn't easy for my friends Kyle and Terra to see God in the empty shell of their home that burned down recently. It isn't easy to see God's motives and plans in the uncertainty of cancer. It isn't easy for a mother to see God's mercy and love in the pain of a miscarriage. It isn't easy to see God's provision when you lose your job. But as painful and confusing as these things are, we don't have to despair. In times like these, we must acknowledge that our eyesight is clouded and beg God to show us His unseen goodness and wisdom.

Disease, death, and disasters are never good. But we can trust that God will always do two things. First, He will give us strength to endure difficulty, and, second, He will use it for good within His perfect plan—to create the greatest good for the greatest number of people over the greatest length of time using the best means possible.[4] I cannot pretend to understand why He allows some things to occur, but I can trust the God who sees and understands and is working all things toward an abundantly good end.

God didn't create a fallen world. He is an active sustainer of all that is good. He will never allow His children to endure pain without ultimately bringing healing and restoration. He will never take something from us without giving us something much better. He will turn every bad thing that happens to us into good.

He will never waste difficulty without accomplishing all the good He desires.

One day, we'll get to heaven and see His glory in all its fullness without the limitations of our self-centeredness or Satan's distortions. We will discover the full mountain range of God's attributes, and we'll look at each other with awe and say, "I had *no* idea!" It will be an honor to express to Jesus our adoration and appreciation; we'll never want to stop. We'll finally be able to acknowledge with all our hearts that everything He did or permitted was part of an ultimately perfect plan. Paul explained it like this: *"For now we see in a mirror dimly, but then face to face; now I know in part, but then I will know fully"* (1 Corinthians 13:12).

TO KNOW HIM IS TO LOVE HIM

I have not avoided adultery because I love rules. I have been faithful in my marriage because my wife, Jan, is so wonderful. My sincere love of pleasing her keeps me from straying from her. Similarly, until we see how incredible our God is, it will be very hard to motivate ourselves to follow Him. No one gets fired up about God because they have to or because they think they should or because their pastor makes them feel guilty if they don't.

The only thing that will fuel our desire for friendship with God over a lifetime is the recognition that He is indescribably amazing. We need to see more and more of the truth about Him: how He feels when He looks at us, His devotion to give us His best, the depth of His wisdom, the greatness of His power, and how arresting His nature is. Seeing and savoring the truth about God's character is the only lasting motivator for walking with

Him. We simply will not pursue a God who is small, irrelevant, uninterested, unhappy with us, or weak.

I am convinced it is impossible to respond poorly to God once we see that He is truly present and active, limitless in power, perfect in wisdom, thinking about us every moment since the beginning of time, and expressing the love of a devoted Father. How could we fail to want fellowship with God if we perceive Him to be relentlessly affectionate, honest, sincere, and caring? How could we doubt One who is perfectly loving and holy in every way at every moment? Why wouldn't we adore One who wants to spend eternity with us because He likes our company?

Even in disappointment, grief, and difficulty, God is always there for us and will never fail us or leave us alone. He wants to use everything bad in our lives for good. His only purpose for His commandments is to ensure what is best for us. When we learn to recognize His hand in our circumstances, we see His abundant mercy and sovereignty in success and failure, in joy and heartache, in health and sickness.

>> How could we fail to want fellowship with God if we perceive Him to be relentlessly affectionate, honest, sincere, and caring? >>

The best part of being a follower of Jesus is getting to see this kind of majesty. The more we see God's true nature and character clearly, the more we will be transformed to be like His Son, which is the best thing that could possibly happen to us. You may have been taught that eternal life is God's greatest gift to us, but that simply isn't true. Seeing Him is our only source of true life and joy. And seeing the truth about Him with increasing dimension will make us ready to enter heaven when the time comes (see 1 John 3:2).

Until then, walking with God is a rhythm of seeing and responding. Seeing Him clearly is a vital first step. The more we see God, the more we will be able to respond well to Him. The next chapter will explore how responding with a growing *confidence* in Him moves us in the direction of paradise.

RESPONDING TO GOD SUGGESTIONS

Consider committing yourself to reading one big idea about the goodness and greatness of God every day. Start in the Psalms, perhaps with Psalm 145. Read each verse until a new thought about God comes to mind. Hold that truth about God's character in your mind until the implications for how it would elevate your view of Him are clear. Ask Him, "Lord, if I really believed this truth, how would my life be different?" Then tell God how much you admire Him for that attribute.

See if you can remember where God's hand was revealed to you in the events of today or yesterday. Where did you have safe travel, provision, a good idea, favor with a person, or help with a project? Then thank Him for revealing Himself to you in that way.

Go to www.morethanordinary.org to see a list of some of God's attributes.

CHAPTER SIX

GREAT EXPECTATIONS

Responding to God with active confidence

We had gathered in our living room, as we did every week, to talk with a group of friends about life with God. But this night was different. We watched in shock as our normally upbeat fifty-something friend (I'll call him David) wept openly. He was a regular church attender and had become familiar with biblical truths through his own daily reading and the thousands of sermons he'd listened to since he was a young boy. It was hard to find a verse he hadn't read or memorized. Yet he'd had only a few meaningful experiences with Jesus in his entire life. He longed for a richer experience in engaging God but had resigned himself to the idea that while others could walk closely with

God, it just wasn't possible for him. His best hope, he believed, for real joy in a relationship with God was to wait until he got to heaven. I think he joined our group for social connection, but even that was hindered by his embarrassment at what he perceived as his spiritual inferiority.

For some time, we had been studying the ideas that form the foundation for this book. In previous gatherings, we'd considered God's passionate desire to help us encounter Him in the full range of life experiences. We discussed the rhythm of walking with God by seeing and responding to Him throughout each day. Everyone seemed excited to think that such a life was possible, and we were all eager to get traction in our daily experiences. We had concluded that our vision of who God is and what life with Him can be like was much too small. There was more paradise to experience in this life than we had believed possible.

Most recently, we'd begun to look at five ways to respond to God, the first being walking by faith. We'd been startled to recognize how vague and abstract "walking by faith" was for us, and we imagined the same was true for most of our friends. It had been reduced to a nice idea that had little to do with real life.

Passing on one of the insights God had been teaching me in that season, I had suggested that we think of a step of faith as expecting God to be who He says He is or to do what He promises to do in a specific life situation and allowing that to change our response to Him. Trusting our Friend and King means we *act* as though His statements in His Word are true. As James, the half brother of Jesus, said, a truth about God must change our attitude or behavior; simply knowing the truth is of no value. Faith that does not propel a positive response to God in a situation is useless. James said it thus: *"Even so faith, if it has no works, is dead, being by itself"* (2:17).

As we talked, I realized something I'd never thought of before that evening. I told my friends that for every one of my forty years since high school, God had been mentoring me in how to live based on four essential truths. He'd been faithfully showing me that He is always present with me in every circumstance (see Psalm 139:7-17), that regardless of how I feel He always desires what is best for me (see Psalm 23:6), that He delights in me and finds infinite joy in fellowship with me (see Psalm 149:4), and that He is the sovereign and supreme Ruler of the universe (see Daniel 2:20-21; 4:34-37). Even though the Bible contains dozens of other truths, these have been the focus and the foundation of my life with God. Every day I learn new implications of what it means to live in light of the truth of these statements.

>> Think of a step of faith as expecting God to be who He says He is or to do what He promises to do in a specific life situation and allowing that to change your response to Him. >>

As we parted, we agreed to start each day of the week ahead by writing down what we expected God to do or be for us *that day* based on specific promises from the Bible. Then, at the end of each day, we'd record how approaching the day with confident expectation of the truth made us see God and our lives differently.

Now we had gathered a week later to describe the results of this exercise, and David, the most reserved person in the group, instantly asked if he could go first. That's when he lost it. He sobbed before a room full of confused but sympathetic friends. Then, composing himself, he told us how this simple exercise had dramatically changed his concept of God and life with Him in a few short days.

David described entering a meeting at work remembering God's promise to give wisdom when we ask (see James 1:5). He asked for wisdom and expected God to give it. His confidence in God to keep His promise changed the meeting for him. Ideas came to him that he would not have otherwise had.

Several other times that week, David returned to the promise for wisdom and was excited to see God help him. When someone came up with a perfect solution to a problem, David thanked God for the wisdom He had provided through a colleague. For the first time in his life, he was attentive to God, expecting Him to act in a context other than church. He couldn't believe what he'd been missing.

David went on nonstop for another thirty minutes, telling us how various experiences at home and at work were transformed when he actively trusted God's promises and statements about Himself. He called it the best week of his life. God's presence became real to him, and his desire for more of God increased dramatically.

David's tears were bittersweet. They expressed his joy in experiencing companionship and adventure with Jesus for the first time. But they also expressed his grief and remorse over what he'd missed by not living this way sooner. He regretted living so long with only a mental library of inert biblical truths that he'd never activated by believing they were true in a specific circumstance. I will never forget his comment at the end of that evening: "I just never thought about confidently expecting God to be or do *anything* before now."

My friend had begun a whole new life with God in which every day could be a great adventure. His faith was no longer academic and inert. It became active, dynamic, and full of confident expectation. That same life is possible for any of us at any time.

TURNING ON THE LIGHTS

Throughout the Bible, God makes bold and powerful statements about Himself and life with Him. Each one is disruptive to ordinary, status quo living. Some of the things He says in His Word tell us what kind of Person He will be for us. Believing these truths about God changes how we see ourselves and our circumstances and propels us to relate to Him differently. He also makes a host of extravagant promises that we can rely on in any life situation. From Genesis to Revelation, God never stops reminding us how valuable we are to Him, how much He delights in us, and how He will never leave us. In addition, His Word is full of extraordinary insights into how life works and what's really important. It reveals that He means life to be an adventure instead of drudgery for us. These stories, proverbs, and commands have the power to help us avoid most of the pain we would otherwise bring on ourselves.

None of this exists merely to educate us. God is not a Divine Professor wanting to fill our minds with information and then testing us to see if we grasp the concepts. He doesn't just want to *inform* us that He is always present with us; He wants the truth that He's crazy about us to revolutionize our relationship with Him. Each truth presents to us a clear fork in the road. Will we trust His truths in the life situations He gives us and act on them, or will we disbelieve or forget them? There is no neutral response to God's truth.

What we really believe in any moment is revealed by how we live. Yesterday, even though I have committed to losing weight,

I devoured a big handful of chocolate chips. In my head, I acknowledge that the best life possible includes being healthy. But in that moment, I chose to believe that the momentary pleasure of candy was worth more than the long-term pleasure of being in shape. I acted on what I *really* believed in that moment, even though I *wanted* to believe differently.

Similarly, every action, attitude, and response to God is colored by what we believe about Him and about what is the best possible life. Every time we respond with confidence in some truth about His character, God *turns on the lights to a far superior reality* in which He towers over everything. The difference between seeing Him in the light and living in the dark about Him is one of the most important metaphors God gives us for life with Him.

John, the close friend of Jesus, chose this imagery when he wrote to some early believers: *"If we say that we have fellowship with Him and yet walk in the darkness, we lie and do not practice the truth; but if we walk in the Light as He Himself is in the Light, we have fellowship with one another, and the blood of Jesus His Son cleanses us from all sin"* (1 John 1:6-7). Note the warning against pretending to live in the light of God's presence and character when we are actually indifferent and independent of Him. On the other hand, to live genuinely in the light of God's character brings enormous benefit to us.

When we go through our day with confidence in His greatness and goodness, expecting Him to be and do what He promises, we'll see our circumstances very differently. This reminds me of a simple analogy: When Jan and I return home after being out for the evening, our first priority is to turn on the lights. It keeps us from groping in the dark, tripping over furniture or each other. In the same way, walking in the light of God's character prevents us from stumbling over every unpleasant circumstance or groping our way through every project or activity. It broadens our field of vision and lifts our focus from accomplishing a project, goal, or agenda to the greater purpose of seeing and responding to God in every moment of the day.

>> Every time we respond with confidence in some truth about His character, God turns on the lights to a far superior reality in which He towers over everything. >>

When we walk in the light, we walk with confidence. Our eyes are opened to see how much better it is to trade our will for His and to trust His leadership over our own. We recognize Him as the most interesting and desirable Person we could ever know and follow. Confidence in God brings great inner strength that allows us to overcome enemies and obstacles to progress in the adventure of following Him. It helps us reject lies suggesting that God is indifferent or inattentive or lies tricking us to believe we would be better off trusting our own counsel. When we walk with Him in the light of truth, we experience more paradise with each passing year. Confidence in God's promises is the switch that connects heaven's power to our daily life.

In contrast, living with the lights turned off means we evaluate everything in terms of what we can see with our physical eyes. This results in low expectations of God. We go through the day with little consideration of His role in our activities, little thought of His desires, and little attention to His personality. We tackle life in our own wisdom, leaning on our strength alone to endure. As we make decisions and navigate difficulties, we remain in the dark regarding God's plans and leadership even though they are always better than what we could come up with on our own. Low expectations of God's character rob us of spiritual desire and make walking with God impossible. They lead to worry, boredom, and anger.

God gave us His Word as a vast treasure of truth. Every truth and every promise must not be simply read but actively trusted in specific situations. Thank God we have all the resources of heaven at our disposal as the Holy Spirit leads us, empowers us, guides us, and encourages us along the way.

David described the transformational character of God's Word this way:

> *The law of the LORD is perfect, restoring the soul;*
> *The testimony of the LORD is sure, making wise the simple.*
> *The precepts of the LORD are right, rejoicing the heart;*
> *The commandment of the LORD is pure, enlightening the eyes.*
> *The fear of the LORD is clean, enduring forever;*
> *The judgments of the LORD are true; they are righteous altogether.*
> *They are more desirable than gold, yes, than much fine gold;*
> *Sweeter also than honey and the drippings of the honeycomb.*
> *Moreover, by them Your servant is warned;*
> *In keeping them there is great reward.* (Psalm 19:7-11)

David was talking about living with the lights turned on all the way in our lives. He was describing how knowing who God is transforms us from the inside out.

LEARNING TO WALK

Walking by faith is taking a series of steps in confident expectation regarding the daily situations we encounter over the entire course of our lives. While I have no slick formula for how we can do this in all the situations life brings our way, I can describe a few practices that help me walk by faith.

The first habit I've tried to cultivate is to **press the pause button** before a meeting, a project, or any activity and ask myself, *What can I expect God to be for me in this event?* or *How has He promised to help me in this situation?* Resetting my expectations of Him has transformed many of the most boring tasks and meetings because I am now engaging God in them. I might remind myself of His presence, His sovereign activity over the outcome of the event, or how He stores up good things for me. I might remember His promise to give me wisdom, to provide for me, to answer every prayer according to His perfect plan, or to give me strength to have the right attitude.

When I go on an important sales call where the outcome seems critical to our business success, I reset my expectation that God is in control of the outcome and that He will do that which is perfectly wise and best for me in the long run. With that perspective in place, I can relax, interact with God in the meeting, and thank Him ahead of time for whatever outcome He desires. In fact, thanking God ahead of time for the way any challenge, problem, or situation will ultimately be resolved is a great step of faith.

Your life may not look much like mine, but whether your work is bagging groceries, running a corporation, raising kids, or anything in between, God loves to participate in it with you.

Before reading the Bible I try to reset my expectations to remember that the Holy Spirit will guide me into truth, illumine the Scriptures so I can understand them, and then empower me to live them. This creates an expectation that God will speak to me personally and that the Holy Spirit will powerfully influence me so I can hear His voice. Resetting my expectations of God turns on the lights for me and allows me to see a far greater reality.

You can do this any time and in any situation. Simply remind yourself of His character or of a particular promise He makes to you and then expect Him to be or do what He says. Does that seem too simplistic? The fact is, we easily forget what we know to be true, and we need a constant stream of reminders of who God is and how He promises to help us.

A second way I walk by faith is to **read the Bible with a transformational lens** rather than an informational lens. This is what I was talking about earlier when I warned against viewing God as a Divine Professor. Rather than looking for God to inform me through the stories, thoughts, and commands in His Word, I ask Him to bring about a fundamental shift in my perspective on life and in how I relate to Him.

When I read a statement about God, for example, I ask Him how my life would be different if I actually believed it to be true. Then I wait for a moment to see what thoughts come into my mind. Take Romans 11:33-34, for example: *"Oh, the depth of the riches both of the wisdom and knowledge of God! How unsearchable are His judgments and unfathomable His ways! For WHO HAS KNOWN THE MIND OF THE LORD, OR WHO BECAME HIS COUNSELOR?"*

Suppose I actually believed His wisdom was this great. How would my life change? After reflecting on this recently, I thanked God for the tapestry of my life that He planned in advance for me. I told Him I wanted to trust and follow His leadership more in my business decisions and to ask for His help more often, having been reminded that the wisest Person in the universe is always sitting next to me and that He loves to give me wisdom when I ask.

If you ask the Spirit how He wants you to live differently according to this verse, His answer may not be the same as what

He showed me. He will apply the same truth in a way that makes sense for your circumstances, personality, and past experiences. The important thing is learning to listen and then letting God transform your heart and mind by believing His Word and acting upon it.

A third practice that helps me walk with God in faith involves **memorizing Scripture** so that I can recall it during the day. Amid the pressure of a situation when I need to know a promise from God or a truth about Him, I often find myself unable to recall much truth unless I have memorized it. Even more important, I find that bringing to mind exactly what the Holy Spirit said is more powerful than my vague recollection of the truth. Memorizing Scripture makes that kind of recall possible.

Can you imagine the impact on your walk with God if you memorized one of God's promises or one bold claim about His character each month for the next ten years? You would have a powerful set of truths at your disposal that could elevate your walk with God beyond your imagination!

WHEN TRIALS COME

Perhaps the greatest challenge to our confidence in God occurs when we are disappointed or even devastated by something hurtful that God permits. In such times we are tempted either to sit in judgment of God's wisdom for allowing the trial or to question His power for not stopping it. We may even doubt that His motives are truly for our best. We cannot understand what is happening, so we question what we once were convinced was true. Yet trusting His unseen goodness and wisdom in times of difficulty is a crucial part of walking with Him.

Let's face it: We are all convinced at a deep level that God is doing His job only when He keeps us from pain and disappointment. This is deeply etched into human nature. But there is a basic inconsistency in how we think. If we were diagnosed with a major heart condition, we would ask a surgeon to do the necessary surgery to heal our condition knowing that the recovery would be painful. And the surgeon would accept the assignment knowing that the benefits would far outweigh the momentary pain. The surgery would generally improve our life and allow us a few more decades with family and friends. We would accept the necessity of the pain even though we also know that surgeons are only human and make mistakes. Why, then, do we struggle to trust our perfect and infallible heavenly Surgeon, who allows pain only for our welfare, to bring spiritual healing to our hearts so we can enjoy more paradise and receive more reward for eternity?

This should give us a different perspective on God's leadership in the circumstances—good or bad—that He allows in our lives. They are for our best ultimately, even if pain or disappointment is involved. And remember, He will never lead us through hardship without giving us all the power we need to endure it. There are good reasons for everything He allows to happen to us.

Our confidence in God is like a muscle that needs resistance to stay healthy and not atrophy. Strange as it may sound, disappointments, difficulties, injustice, financial failures, disease, and even the death of loved ones have the power to strengthen our trust in God when we choose to believe His Word rather than giving in to feelings that fluctuate with mood and circumstances. An easy life, in contrast, tempts us to be cold and indifferent to God by tricking us into thinking we don't really need Him. That's when atrophy sets in.

Trials make it difficult to believe the truth about God and trust His unseen goodness, power, and wisdom. A war rages deep in our minds and hearts. On the one hand, we have the simple, straightforward truth sourced in God's own words. On the other, we face lies that come at us from all kinds of places: our own minds, the world around us, or the Evil One. During trials the Devil works overtime to take advantage of our disappointment and convince us of falsehoods about God's character and plan. To combat such lies, Paul told his spiritual son Timothy, *"Fight the good fight of faith"* (1 Timothy 6:12). Paul knew that believing God is sometimes a battle.

>> Disappointments, difficulties, injustice, financial failures, disease, and even the death of loved ones have the power to strengthen our trust in God when we choose to believe His Word rather than giving in to feelings that fluctuate with mood and circumstances. >>

When I remember the difficult experiences of my life, my heart is exposed in a way that is humbling but ultimately good. Reflecting on some of these trials has revealed recurring errors in my thinking about God. At times I've said, "God, You are wrong not to give me what I know I deserve." The pronouns are very telling; my arrogance in judging God's wisdom and motives makes me cringe. I've also said things such as, "God, I really love You and try to obey You more than other people I know. Why don't You bless me like You've blessed them?" But I am not better than anyone else, and any good motives and desires I have are because He empowered me to have them. I've also told God more than once, "This is unfair and I don't deserve it. Why haven't

You fixed it?" I have died to my rights and my agenda many times, and I want to live for Him, yet that kind of living for God and dying to self is a lifelong process, and pain exposes my true level of surrender at any given time.

Last year, a business I started and led for fifteen years fell on hard times two years after I retired from it. As a result, the business was not able to pay Jan and me our retirement. Believe me, I know that this pales in light of the persecution, torture, and even martyrdom that my brothers and sisters around the world are facing. Still, it was scary thinking we might not have the income we need when I can no longer work. To trust God amid financial turmoil is a battle for me. Some days, I have to combat fear many times with God's promises of provision and protection.

You'll have similar struggles. You will have to fight anger at others and at God by remembering that He is sovereign and supreme and that He allows trials for good purposes. You will find enormous freedom in echoing what Joseph said to his brothers years after they betrayed him in the worst possible way. Recognizing God's purpose for allowing their betrayal, Joseph told his brothers, *"You meant evil against me, but God meant it for good in order to bring about this present result, to preserve many people alive"* (Genesis 50:20).

You'll have to choose to surrender to His will when you don't understand it. You'll have to stay confident in His promises to give you strength to overcome the bonds of self-love. But it's worth it. The only time a difficult situation becomes a true tragedy is when a person chooses to become bitter toward God. *Long-term bitterness toward God is a thousand times more destructive than any trial you could face.*

As hard as it may be, steadfastly trusting God's plans and

purposes through storms will bring unimaginable rewards in this life and throughout eternity. *"For momentary, light affliction is producing for us an eternal weight of glory far beyond all comparison, while we look not at the things which are seen, but at the things which are not seen; for the things which are seen are temporal, but the things which are not seen are eternal"* (2 Corinthians 4:17-18). None of your struggles and none of your pain will ever be wasted.

GOD IS PREDICTABLE; CIRCUMSTANCES ARE NOT

While we're talking about trials, I want to stress a critical truth: *God will always be predictable in terms of the kind of Person He will be for us. But circumstances are not predictable to us.* This is a vital distinction to make. Regardless of how it seems, God will always be present, active, and perfectly devoted to giving us paradise in Him. He will always be kind in everything He does. He will always be generously committed to what is ultimately best for us and for others. He will never lie or fail to keep a promise. He doesn't change in the slightest degree; He is entirely unlike us in this way.

One of my favorite books is A. W. Tozer's *The Knowledge of the Holy.* In it, he makes the powerful point that God has a brilliant plan to accomplish the greatest good for the greatest number of people over the greatest amount of time using the best means possible. Sometimes it is easy to see the goodness of God. He loves giving good gifts to people. We always know in any situation what kind of Person He will be for us and what He will do to help us. But He will also allow difficult things to occur for His good purposes. This means that while we can be utterly confident about what kind of Person God is, we will rarely be able to predict the circumstances God will bring our way. God crafts our circumstances with amazing intentionality. Everything has a purpose, and every purpose is monumentally good.

Knowing this means life will always be an adventure. How will He use us, speak to us, lead us, or empower us to stand in the storms of difficulty? We won't know the specifics beforehand, but we can cultivate confidence in His character and look forward to the ways He'll ultimately use all things for good.

When I am nervous about the future, it helps me to remember that God has determined the outcome. An anchor verse for me is this: *"The LORD reigns, let the earth rejoice"* (Psalm 97:1). Whatever happens, God reigns and His reign is filled with His goodness. We can celebrate ahead of time the amazing and wonderful things God will do because He is in complete control and has perfectly good plans for everything. There are infinite reasons why God does what He does and permits what He does—reasons my finite mind cannot grasp, but reasons that are always good. If God decides to take something from us, He will give us something better. He may allow us to lose a job in order to give us a greater trust in Him and love for Him—and maybe, of second importance, the gift of a better job too. But please don't forget which of these will last forever. In ten thousand years, a better job won't matter, but a stronger friendship with God will. When God allows pain, it is often to bring healing of some kind to our hearts or minds, and it is always ultimately for good. When God permits difficulty, He will never fail to be with us in it and to supply all the strength we need to endure it.

MISTRUST IS TOXIC

Like Adam and Eve before us, we are all prone to be cynical toward God at times. Everyone has laughed skeptically at God's promises as Sarah did. You probably remember the story. God promised Abraham and Sarah they would have a child. As the years went by Sarah waited for God to keep His word in His time. Finally, when she and Abraham were both nearly one hundred years old, God appeared to them with the great news that within a year they would have a child.

Sarah's heart had grown cold toward God, so when she heard Him make this promise,

> *Sarah laughed to herself, saying, "After I have become old, shall I have pleasure, my lord being old also?" And the* LORD *said to Abraham, "Why did Sarah laugh, saying, 'Shall I indeed bear a child, when I am so old?' Is anything too difficult for the* LORD*? At the appointed time I will return to you, at this time next year, and Sarah will have a son."*
> (Genesis 18:12-14)

Years of the month-after-month cycle of hope and crushing disappointment had gotten to Sarah. I have been there, and I bet you have too. Her laugh represents the attitude of all of us who examine the promises of God and His statements about His character and say, "Yeah, right!" It is so easy to drift into skepticism.

But mistrust and cynicism will contaminate any friendship. Imagine how much it would hurt if your closest friend didn't trust you to tell the truth, keep a promise, or be loyal. You would take it very personally. So does God. The damage that comes from not believing Him is far worse than the damage caused by not trusting someone else who is worthy of your confidence. Unbelief is the worst disease on the face of the earth. It leads to ruined lives, wrecked relationships, fear, stress, anger, and deep insecurity. Choosing not to believe God—calling Him a liar openly or deep inside your heart and mind—can open the door to all kinds of evil. Unchecked skepticism will lead to permanently walking away from God, as Scripture tells us so many followers of Jesus have done: *"Take care, brethren, that there not be in any one of you an evil, unbelieving heart that falls away from the living God"* (Hebrews 3:12).

>> Unbelief is the worst disease on the face of the earth. It leads to ruined lives, wrecked relationships, fear, stress, anger, and deep insecurity. >>

One of the most pivotal moments in Israel's history occurred as the people prepared to enter the Promised Land. They had traveled to a place called Kadesh Barnea, and they were told to trust God's leadership and enter the land He promised them. Up to this point, His people had experienced countless miraculous expressions of God's love and power as they left Egypt and lived in the desert. But now, seeing how formidable the enemies were in this new land, the Israelites accused God of bringing them to this point only to let them be destroyed. They doubted the single most important element of God's character: His desire to give them His best. Tragically, their unbelief prevented that generation from ever entering the Promised Land. They missed the incredible life God wanted to give them because they chose to trust their own instincts over God's promises.

Stubborn and continual unbelief can rob us of the rich life, the great adventure, and the incredible legacy God wants to give us, just as it robbed this generation of Israel. We need a holy fear of ruining our lives through doubt or unbelief.

No one in heaven will ever catch God telling a lie or failing to keep a single promise. Not for one second of all eternity. We will all fail to be loyal to Him, but He will never be anything but trustworthy to all humankind. Unlike us, He is never fickle and never tells a half-truth. The Bible assures us that *"God is not a man, that He should lie, nor a son of man, that He should repent; has He said, and will He not do it? Or has He spoken, and will He not make it good?"* (Numbers 23:19). I wonder how different our lives could be if we lived as if God was *this* reliable.

CULTIVATING CONFIDENCE IN GOD

Any event or circumstance can be transformed by simply expecting God to be as amazing, powerful, friendly, wise, loyal, devoted, loving, and fatherly as He says He is. Living this out on a daily basis is a journey. No one does it perfectly all at once. A habit of walking by faith won't happen overnight. Every day we miss opportunities to have great expectations of God because we simply forget or because we doubt. But the more we take even the smallest steps, the more we turn on the lights to the real world. Each day opens the possibility of a great adventure in trusting His promises and considering every command a path to paradise.

Much of the trajectory of our lives is made up of seemingly small, daily decisions. This is true for diet and exercise, for budgeting and saving, and in career and family choices. And it's true for our walk with God. Enjoying life with Him happens as we make decisions to involve Him in our lives as they unfold day by day. The more we confidently expect God to be or do what He says in a situation, the more paradise we will enjoy, both now and for all eternity. Confident expectation is one of the major steps we take in walking with God. I don't want a single one of you reading this book to miss any of the extraordinary life God is eager to give you. My prayer for you is that you'll start making more small decisions to be confident in God's character. And I'll make you a promise: The more you choose to trust Him, the more you'll see that He is *abundantly* trustworthy. Every active and deliberate step of faith will bring more paradise. It is an essential part of enjoying a friendship with God and allows us to live in a greater reality with a very big God!

RESPONDING TO GOD SUGGESTIONS

Take a situation in your life that is frustrating, unfair, or scary and write down all the promises and truths of what God will do and who He will be for you in that situation. You may list things like: He will always be loyal, devoted, in control, present, perfectly wise, infinitely good; He will supply all the strength; He will answer every prayer; and so on. Then ask God how really believing His words would change your heart and mind in the situation.

Another possibility is to stop before you begin a project, meeting, conversation, or any activity and reflect on this question: "What do I expect God to be or do in this situation?"

CHAPTER SEVEN

THE CONVERSATION

Responding to God by processing life with Him

There are two conversations I can't imagine living without. One is with my wife, Jan, at the end of the day. For reasons I can't explain fully, if I don't get this time with her because of travel or guests in our home, I feel out of sorts. Our talks are more vital to my sanity today than when we were first married thirty-six years ago. I'm convinced they are one reason we have grown in our love for each other over the years.

We both look forward to the part of the day when we get to sit down together and process our day or, if necessary, get caught up on the last few days. We usually start with mundane facts about what we did or what happened to us, but soon we drift into deeper issues of how things made us feel or how we interacted with God in our circumstances. Because we care deeply about each other, we want to know what the other is fearful of, angry about, or frustrated with. We want to know what is going on in the other's mind and heart and how the other is doing in his or her relationship with Jesus.

We are mentors to one other as we talk. Often in our conversations, Jan will advise me in how to raise our daughter and love her well. She has also helped me understand the feelings of our boys. In return, I believe I have helped her understand childrearing from a father's point of view.

Our conversations also give us perspective on problems. Sometimes we see that issues looming large in our minds aren't so big. Or maybe what we thought was a small issue was significant after all. I can't tell you how many times I have mentioned something about work that seemed trivial only to find that Jan saw a bigger problem and helped me address it before it got worse. She is incredibly insightful, and I make few major decisions at work or home without her input.

We love to celebrate small victories together where we've seen God's good gifts during the day. Processing together the amazing things we saw God do, say, and reveal—or the ways He used us to help others—has built a bond between us that continues to grow. The greatest things we share in common are our love for Jesus and our love for our family.

I use our talks to encourage Jan. Calling out what I admire and appreciate in her and noting the noble things she does is life-giving for both of us. Jan and I can be hard on ourselves for mistakes we make. Our conversations provide an antidote to that destructive tendency. They rekindle our affection for each other, align our hearts, and give us a sense of partnering in everything. They change us.

All of us need healthy, encouraging, open, and honest

dialogue with friends and family. But we may not realize how much we need the same thing with a vastly greater Person. *That* is the second conversation I can't imagine living without. My need for conversation with God is even greater than my need to converse with Jan. He created us for conversation; He longs for us to process life with Him verbally. And He passionately desires for us to listen as He speaks directly to us, with great affection, in the midst of daily activity.

GOD LOVES TALKING WITH US

That God loves to listen to us and speak to us makes sense to me because God is a Father. I know how much satisfaction I find in talking with my kids. I love to give them my best counsel and, as a result, see them encouraged and helped. I love hearing about their days, their challenges, their victories, and their disappointments. I want to know how they are doing with Jesus. But as with any human analogy, my love for conversing with my kids as compared to God's zeal for talking with us is as a speck of dust compared to the entire universe.

Paul summed up God's invitation to conversation this way: *"Rejoice always; pray without ceasing; in everything give thanks; for this is God's will for you in Christ Jesus"* (1 Thessalonians 5:16-18). The conversation God has in mind for us is interspersed naturally throughout the day as we live with our heavenly Father. He designs each day to be full of opportunities for rich dialogue with Him. Talking to Him can be as simple and real as what I told Him recently: "Lord, I am so embarrassed by what I just said!" We don't get extra points for long, eloquent, or theologically impressive prayers. In fact, there is no point system. God wants us to enjoy deep companionship with Him. He wants us to say what we're thinking. He wants us to tell Him how we need His help or what we admire about Him as we drive to work, complete the day's project, or talk to our spouses. I've experienced this kind of multitasking with God. It is amazing how talking with Him as I go makes whatever I am doing better.

Whenever I am unclear what to do with God, I start talking to Him. Often, I picture the Father, Son, and Holy Spirit leaning forward together to hear what I'm about to say. Beginning the dialogue is a tipping point that moves my heart from indifference to interest, from being stressed to relaxing in His strength, and from feeling alone in fighting the giants in the land to a deeper level of companionship with Him and confidence in His strength. I know that God loves it when I talk to Him. I know that I desperately need these conversations to live sanely. Every time I talk to Him, it is a trade up for me.

>>   Whenever I am unclear what to do with God, I start talking to Him. Often, I picture the Father, Son, and Holy Spirit leaning forward together to hear what I'm about to say. >>

Conversing with God in this way is not easy to wrap our minds around. Many people balk at the logic of it. How can God simultaneously maintain the universe, know every star by name, keep track of every hair on every head, and also talk with each of His children? But He can. He is God. He doesn't share our limitations. It is as the prophet Jeremiah described: *"Ah Lord GOD! Behold, You have made the heavens and the earth by Your great power and by Your outstretched arm! Nothing is too difficult for You"* (Jeremiah 32:17).

Others mistakenly think they are honoring God by sparing Him the details of the small stuff of daily life. They believe it is better to talk to Him only about the important things. They worry that their comparatively small concerns can rob the Father's attention from others who need Him more. But that isn't the way it works. He cares about each of His children down to the smallest detail. That's why Scripture tells us to ask Him for things we need or desire. Notice Jesus' clear logic that because He loves us and wants the best for us, we should ask Him for good things in any situation:

Ask, and it will be given to you; seek, and you will find; knock, and it will be opened to you. For everyone who asks receives, and he who seeks finds, and to him who knocks it will be opened. Or what man is there among you who, when his son asks for a loaf, will give him a stone? Or if he asks for a fish, he will not give him a snake, will he? If you then, being evil, know how to give good gifts to your children, how much more will your Father who is in heaven give what is good to those who ask Him! (Matthew 7:7-11)

God commands us to ask Him for help, and as with every other commandment, it is for our best. He derives great pleasure when we trust His leadership by doing in faith what He asks us to do. We are never bothering God with the details of our lives. Rather, talking with Him about every aspect of our lives is an act of obedience and an expression of our trust in Him.

Whatever our reasons, it is understandable that we would feel insecure in talking to God. He is so utterly different from us, so thoroughly holy, righteous, and pure. We are adopted into His family, but most of us have a long way to go toward achieving a family resemblance. We know the backstage versions of ourselves. We know how often we resist His leadership, ignore Him, and fail to walk with Him.

That's where the Cross comes into play. Until we believe wholeheartedly that Jesus' sacrifice paid the full price for us to be completely and forever accepted by God as His children and loved with the same kind of love He has for His Son, we will remain insecure. We'll be reluctant to run into His presence and talk to Him.

But God wants us to be confident in His welcome, no matter what. We are His beloved children. He has given us an invitation and a right to ask for His help on behalf of ourselves and others. He wants us to talk with Him about what's happening to us today and about our dreams and hopes for the future. There is nothing we can't respectfully tell Him. He listens with compassion when we describe our deepest hurts, what we're struggling with, and where our faith is weak.

I loved it that my kids knew they could always enter my office and I would stop whatever I was doing to give them my attention. Similarly, God loves it when we come into His presence as though we belong. He is filled with joy when His children come before Him with confidence, knowing they have a *right* to enter His presence and ask for big things. Because we do, as Scripture so clearly tells us: *"Therefore let us draw near with confidence to the throne of grace, so that we may receive mercy and find grace to help in time of need"* (Hebrews 4:16).

GOD LOVES HONESTY

Not only can we be confident that God enjoys conversation, but we can also be assured that He always appreciates complete honesty and transparency as we process life with Him. He wants us to feel the freedom to talk through the good, the bad, and the ugly with Him. He loves honesty.

God already knows everything inside of me. He can see when I am angry, afraid, lazy, selfish, deceptive, or fearful. Yet my sin and immaturity do not shake His steadfast zeal for connection with me. He feels the same way about you. No one is crazier about you than God. No one loves you as He does. When you really get this, it changes everything. Knowing that He will never reject us paves the way for us to be honest with Him about what we think and feel. Every child of God gets angry with Him at times and questions His motives or plans when difficulty and disappointment occur. We all struggle with impatience with God when we ask Him for help and He seems slow to respond. Conversation with God should be the most open and unguarded that we have with anyone. He doesn't want anything white-washed. The psalmist declared of God, *"Behold, You desire truth in the innermost being"* (Psalm 51:6).

God invites us to talk with Him about whatever we are encountering: finances, relationships, health, family—anything. Because He made us, He knows that talking with Him changes us. He doesn't listen begrudgingly, wishing we'd figure things out so He could move on to what He really wants to do. He meant for us to process life with Him with complete honesty and openness. I believe this is especially hard for Americans, who are used to talking more about our circumstances than about what is in our hearts.

I learned this firsthand in 2002 when I was in Germany

helping a software client with business strategy. After a full day of meetings with the executive in charge of that region, the two of us enjoyed an incredible dinner in Frankfurt. His idea of dinner conversation couldn't have been more different from the shallow discussions I was accustomed to in business settings. He respectfully asked me about things he thought I might care about and was also very open about himself. He spent an hour describing his passion for Italian opera. Far from being bored, I was left wishing for friends back home who would probe beyond the surface of my life.

Americans typically have a low "outer wall" in communication. We tend to smile a lot and are friendly. However, we ask each other how we're doing with no expectation of transparency. Even in close relationships, we rarely share inner fears, insecurities, and dreams. Nor do we tend to ask questions about such topics. Europeans, on the other hand, typically have a high outer wall. A shopkeeper in Berlin, for example, probably won't gush with warmth and friendliness when someone enters his store in the manner that a storeowner in Atlanta would. Yet my European friends are honest and forthright about their true feelings with those they know and trust.

>> God is never offended by our struggles or our feelings. He wants His children to work through their true thoughts and emotions with Him. >>

God is interested in what is behind our *inner* walls, the deepest part of us. He doesn't want a shallow, surface relationship with us.

Not long ago, I was telling Him how much I was struggling to trust His good intentions because of the business and financial pressure He had brought our way. I told Him I really wanted to trust Him but couldn't get my mind and heart in the same place. I confessed the ugly truth of how I felt. It seemed to me He had allowed too much pain and disappointment. I was doubting His commitment to us.

I told Him I didn't like the way He was allowing my plans to be crushed again. I said I was really angry that He was requiring Jan to lay down some of her dreams. And amid all this honesty, something surprising occurred. The more I told God the truth of what was in my heart, the more the conversation allowed the Holy Spirit to change my attitude toward Him. I knew my attitude was wrong. I knew I needed His help to see things differently. Somehow, He provided it. I had peace again, and my confidence in His leadership returned.

God is never offended by our struggles or our feelings. He wants His children to work through their true thoughts and emotions with Him. He loves that. Here is what the Holy Spirit says in Psalm 62:8: *"Trust in Him at all times, O people; pour out your heart before Him; God is a refuge for us."*

John Calvin, the sixteenth-century theologian, pondered this verse and wrote,

> David is . . . exposing that diseased but deeply rooted principle in our nature, which leads us to hide our griefs, and ruminate upon them, instead of relieving ourselves at once by pouring out our prayers and complaints before God. The consequence is that we are distracted more and more with our distresses.[1]

None of us needs to walk through life "distracted . . . with our distresses" when we have a Father who takes pleasure in our honest expression of emotion.

GOD ALWAYS ANSWERS

Some people may concede that God enjoys conversation with us, listens well, and is not offended by our honesty. Yet they believe God is whimsical when it comes to responding to our requests.

The truth is, God always gives exactly what we request or something even better. We read in 1 John, *"This is the confidence which we have before Him, that, if we ask anything according to His will, He hears us. And if we know that He hears us in whatever we ask, we know that we have the requests which we have asked from Him"* (5:14-15).

There simply are no unanswered prayers. No request is ignored or rejected. God may give us what we ask but years later than we expected. Or He may choose to give us something much better than what we asked for. But He always gives us what He knows is best for us in His perfect timing.

A friend of mine had worked in a position for five years, hoping and praying for a promotion to manager. One day, he learned of a managerial opening in San Francisco, and he quickly applied. Two weeks later the position was filled by someone who had never worked for the company. My friend struggled with God for a few weeks over an outcome that seemed unfair. Then three months later, the company shut down the San Francisco office and let the new manager go. If my friend had received that job, he would have moved his family to a new city only to be laid off three months later. He was so thankful that did not happen. He felt as I often feel—silly for questioning God's wisdom—and he was thankful that God did not answer his prayer in the way he had hoped! We simply do not know what is best for us.

I am better able to leave the answers to my prayers in God's hands when I remember that He is simultaneously devoted to my best, infinitely wise, and monumentally powerful. When I trust in His character, I increasingly ask for what *He* wants rather than what I think is best in my limited wisdom. Giving God that kind of control over my life is never easy. I have to hold every desire, goal, and plan with a light touch. I need to give Him full permission to lead me where He will—even if it means disappointment or hardship for a time. I have to echo Jesus' surrender, *"Lord, not my will but Yours be done"* (see Mark 14:36). And I have to renew this commitment every single day.

When I am tempted, even in light of overwhelming evidence to the contrary, to think I know better than God—and to wrest back control from Him—He lovingly reminds me, *"For My thoughts are not your thoughts, nor are your ways My ways. . . . For as the heavens are higher than the earth, so are My ways higher than your ways and My thoughts than your thoughts"* (Isaiah 55:8-9).

God always listens carefully to everything we say. And He will give us what we ask for or something vastly better. I am convinced that believing these two truths will revolutionize our walk with God. We'll want to ask Him for more and to talk to Him more often. And we'll be propelled to thank Him when He sets aside our agendas because we'll know He has something much better for us.

A BETTER REALITY

Conversation with God turns on the lights to a far greater reality. This is especially evident when our conversation focuses on praise and thanksgiving. Appreciating God throughout the day draws me into a bigger world in which I can clearly see that He is greater than my circumstances, my fears, and my problems. Telling Him how much I admire Him reminds me of the incredible truth that my Father is an all-powerful King. Worshiping Him always leads my heart to a much better state. I seem to catch some of the enthusiasm for God that is expressed in heaven. Asking God a question and waiting for an answer aligns my mind and heart with His.

Sometimes we think it's sufficient to *think* big thoughts of God, but we need to do more than that. We need to *speak* to Him of our adoration and appreciation. As C. S. Lewis said, joy is not complete until we verbalize it in praise. When I verbally honor God for who He is, something inside of me that's hungry gets fed, as if I am doing what I was born to do. The more I praise Him throughout the day in various circumstances, the happier I am. Thanking God also gives clarity to His role in my life. It reminds me that every project, every good idea, and every good thing I have comes from His hand and I have the privilege of participating in what He is doing in and through me. If I get to work safely, I am not the one who deserves thanks, though I drive as carefully as possible. Every good idea I have in business, every good thing I do to love Jan and my children, is empowered and sparked by Him. I can say no to Him—He gives me that freedom—but God is the source of every good thing in me.

Expressing gratitude for what He will do in the future puts practical feet to the idea of expecting great things of God. When I am nervous about a meeting, I try to thank God ahead of time for His perfect plan and how He will control the results of the meeting. I try to look forward to unseen solutions He will bring at just the right time, to strength He will give, and to surprising expressions of His love and kindness. It is right to anticipate His faithfulness because He will never let any of His children down. Thanking Him ahead of time aligns our hearts with His reality.

I am convinced that our happiness on any given day is directly proportional to the number of times we thank God. Verbalizing our gratitude to Him as we go about the day simultaneously does several good things for our hearts: It allows us to celebrate His goodness; it reminds us of His presence, interest, and activity; it elevates our minds beyond the seen world; and it gives us joy and probably a host of other good things. Some days, it is easy to give Him thanks and honor. Other days, I praise Him through teeth gritted in disappointment.

Praying *for* others keeps us from being self-absorbed and always challenges us. And praying *with* others elevates the level of conversation we can have with God and improves our companionship with the person with whom we are praying.

>> Expressing gratitude for what He will do in the future puts practical feet to the idea of expecting great things of God. >>

To those who don't know me well, I seem to be steady and consistent in my walk with God. Some believe I never struggle in my relationship with Him. But the truth is, a constant battle wages behind the inner wall of my life. Every day I swing back and forth between distraction or self-absorption and loving God. During frustrating or disappointing moments, connecting with God feels like a wrestling match for me.

Please don't think I am exaggerating to make you feel better. I am picturing my wrestling matches in college. Wrestling is intense and involves a constant seesaw as to who is winning. My mind and heart are like that. They teeter back and forth between attitudes that are life-giving and those that bring darkness. On a given day, I can be filled with praise and gratitude one minute and then overcome by fear or anger in the next. I'm embarrassed by how easily I can speak to a crowd with eloquence about trusting God's goodness and then complain about some small matter on the trip home. Throughout every day, I fight to see Him and respond to Him. Every one of His children will fight this battle for the rest of life this side of heaven.

Amid all this tension, talking to God always creates a fundamental shift inside me. It swings me from self-absorption toward loving and enjoying Him. It aligns my mind and heart with His and transforms my worst attitudes into loyalty and gratitude for Him.

ASKING GOD WHAT HE WANTS

It is normal for those who are new at walking with God to ask Him mainly for help with their goals and for relief from their pain. After all, when our kids were babies, they didn't ask for wisdom or understanding. They were hungry and wanted their appetites satisfied right then! In the same way, sometimes Christians get stuck in the infant stage for their whole lives. This is a tragedy. Limiting our conversation with God to listing material needs or asking for help in a crisis will keep us from experiencing the full life God wants to give us.

As we get to know another person, we eventually discover what matters to that person—what she values and what she considers trivial. The same is true in knowing God. Over time, enjoying and walking with Him should result in a heart that increasingly values pleasing Him more than having comfortable or easy circumstances.

What does God value? What pleases Him? God values in His children the kind of faith that expects Him to be and do all that He promises. He wants to give us increasing adventure in place of boring, stoic lives. He is pleased when we lay down our will for His because we know His is always better. He is pleased when we live above our circumstances with peace and courage in the midst of difficulty.

He values what is in our hearts more than whether we do a few good deeds every day. Outward moral behavior without a genuine love and loyalty for Him is of little value to Him. God's ultimate desire is that we enjoy the same kind of relationship with Him that He has with Jesus and exhibit the same responsiveness to Him that Jesus modeled every day on earth. The more we come to see that God values what is best for us, the more we'll cry out to Him for help so that our actions and attitude may be pleasing to Him.

Three particular practices have helped me grow in praying according to what God values, and I've seen them help others as well. First, I encourage you to **let Scripture guide your prayers.** It will bring remarkable spiritual power and insight. Simply read a passage and then use the text as the content of your prayer. The psalms give you words and ideas you can use to offer praise to God. I suggest you start with Psalm 37, 63, or 145. Make the passage personal. As you read and interact with God, be sensitive to any new or fresh revelations of His greatness or goodness that He is trying to impress on you. You can also use this practice with Paul's prayers for the early church. You'll find them in the New Testament epistles. I recommend using Ephesians 1 and 3 and Colossians 1. Ask God to fulfill each element of these prayers for you and your friends.

Second, in any situation (and especially in difficult ones) **ask**

God how you might honor Him with your heart before you ask Him for what you want for yourself. I once had a severe reaction to a prescription drug. I was unable to go to work for three weeks. During that time, I was tempted just to pray for quick healing. But instead I asked God to help me respond well to Him in the situation. I didn't want to miss anything He wanted to give me. Praying that way slowly changed my perspective from self-pity to expectation. Rather than stewing and complaining as I would naturally tend to do, I had a lot more joy. Over the years, I have seen how critical it is for us to ask God to help us respond well to hard circumstances. Counterintuitive as it seems, more joy comes from responding well to God than from getting our way.

A third simple way I've found to honor what God values is to **ask Him to show you what to pray.** Not long ago, my son Matt was going through a difficult time. I woke early one morning and asked God what I should pray for him. I sat quietly with a pen and some paper handy and wrote down the verses and ideas that came to mind. I reread them to make sure they were not simply something I would have come up with on my own. Then I prayed that list of verses and requests for my son every day for more than a year. God answered every prayer in a way I could clearly see. He is good and faithful!

In chapters 8 and 9 you'll find more on how to listen to God's voice. But these three ways of talking to Him are good first—and ongoing—steps for aligning your heart and mind with His.

OXYGEN FOR THE SOUL

The question Jan usually asks me at the end of the day—"How did your day go?"—reveals more than I sometimes realize about how I think, what I value, and the trajectory of my relationship with God. But what if we changed the question a little? What if we asked each other, "What was your conversation with your Father like today? What did you say to Jesus, and what did the Spirit say to you?" I wonder if that would shift us from thinking about better circumstances to enjoying the God of the universe in every realm of life. Might it help us see processing life with God as essential to life—like oxygen?

>> Interaction with God is the oxygen of the soul. Without frequent communication with Him, I get spiritually hypoxic—focused only on the tasks in front of me, unaware of His presence, unable to listen to Him or think clearly. >>

After I graduated from the Air Force Academy, I was an instructor pilot for a few years. During that time I had several in-flight emergencies. The most dangerous one was an oxygen malfunction I discovered at forty thousand feet. Immediately upon discovery, I declared an aircraft emergency with the ground controller and began a very steep and rapid descent. During the descent, the effects of the lack of oxygen began to set in. All my hundreds of hours of flight training couldn't overcome the physical effects of hypoxia. My thinking grew foggy, and I was unable to see anything except what was straight in front of me. I had what pilots call "tunnel vision," as though I were looking down a long tube at a small spot in front of me.

As the controller gave me instructions, my speech began to slur in response because my tongue was swollen from lack of oxygen. Knowing I was drifting into unconsciousness as my fighter plane screamed toward the ground at near supersonic speed, he shouted to me on the radio to try to keep me awake. I was terrified! But when I got to a lower altitude, the air outside the plane contained enough oxygen for me to breathe normally. My sight, speech, and ability to listen to the controller returned. Thank God, I landed safely.

Life with God works in a similar way. *Interaction with God is the oxygen of the soul.* Without frequent communication with Him, I get spiritually hypoxic—focused only on the tasks in front of me, unaware of His presence, unable to listen to Him or think clearly. On the days that I barely talk to God, my relationship with Him seems flat and boring. Without much interaction, I cannot know Him well as a Person or feel much affection for Him. I begin to doubt He is relevant to my life. I miss out on His fatherly mentoring and His encouragement. I breeze past insights into who He is and what that means for my value and worth.

But when I turn toward Him in conversation, I am fully awake and alive again. The more I communicate with God, the more enthusiastic I feel about knowing Him better and following Him. Talking to Him helps me interpret my circumstances from heaven's perspective. Life appears simpler and clearer. I experience more of what He has planned for me. Talking to God changes me as nothing else can and motivates me to respond to Him. The more frequent and deeper my conversation with Him, the better my life is.

Conversation with God is not just a nice idea, an option available for the ultraspiritual. It is essential for anyone who wants to have perspective, energy, and fullness of life with Him. Once you make it a practice of your life, you'll wonder how you ever survived without it.

RESPONDING TO GOD SUGGESTION

Take a moment and tell God honestly how you feel about Him today. Whether you are grateful, happy to know Him, disappointed, or confused, tell Him what change you would like Him to make to your desire to know Him and walk with Him. Ask Him what He would have you do to enjoy Him more. See if these things change your orientation to Him.

Note: For a list of great expectations of God in specific situations, go to www.morethanordinary.org.

CHAPTER EIGHT

TRADING UP

Responding to God's perfect leadership

About a year into a season of spiritual renewal, I had worked my way through the Old Testament filling journal after journal with insights God was giving me about who He is and what life with Him is all about.

In Genesis, God's passion to give us paradise in Him—and the truth that *He* finds paradise in fathering us—amazed me. Exodus opened my eyes to God's steadfast desire to dwell with His people, a passion that weaves a common thread through every story the Bible tells. Studying the lives of Israel's kings revealed the stark contrast between those who walked with God and those who did not. The Psalms proclaimed that we are created to be so awestruck and captivated with the majesty of God that we are utterly transformed by Him. I loved reading Proverbs' moving portrayal of a father taking his son through the city and using what they saw as object lessons for how to relate well to God in every life circumstance. The Prophets exposed the variety of ways humans substitute religion for a true friendship with God.

RESCUE FROM VAGUENESS

Now I was ready to listen to Jesus speak to me from the Gospels, specifically the gospel of John. My goal for this study was to discover a more concrete idea of what it means to be a *follower* of Jesus. It can be such a vague concept. *Surrender, commitment,* and *devotion* are words used frequently in Christian conversation, but what do they really mean? I wanted to fulfill the urgent and sincere statement I made to Jesus at age fourteen when I told Him to take my life and run it. We hear people say they are committed to Christ, but how do they follow Him in the small daily stuff—while having dinner with family, at a soccer game, or in a meeting at work? Finally, I wanted to understand better the notion of wholehearted surrender to God's plan. Why does it seem scary, as though it will make life worse instead of better?

John's gospel is rich with insight into who Jesus is and how He created life to work. One of those insights is found in the life-changing words of John 10: *"The thief comes only to steal and kill and destroy; I came that they may have life, and have it abundantly. I am the good shepherd; the good shepherd lays down His life for the sheep"* (John 10:10-11).

The thief's goal is to destroy God's children. The good Shepherd's purpose is the polar opposite: He loves guiding us into more and more of the abundant life He wants for us. And

He never forgets us or changes His mind about us; He will never let us go. He tells us, *"My sheep hear My voice, and I know them, and they follow Me; and I give eternal life to them, and they will never perish; and no one will snatch them out of My hand"* (John 10:27-28).

Many who read these verses picture nothing more than a docile and kindhearted shepherd with his cuddly sheep. But that is not Jesus' message here. As we will see in a moment, His statements about who He is and who we are represent a radical departure from the religious thought of His day and ours.

THE FLAWLESS LEADER

Our English translation of the original Greek New Testament says that Jesus is "the good shepherd." In our culture, the word *good* can mean anything from spectacular to barely tolerable, depending on the context. But the Greek word translated *good* leaves no room for misunderstanding. Often used by ancient Greek philosophers, it might better be translated "flawless," as in morally perfect or completely competent. It also is the ultimate expression of an excellent character. This distinguishes a leader who is good in an "it'll do" kind of way from one who towers over any other leader in wisdom, devotion, and purity of motives. Thinking about Jesus this way stopped me in my tracks and filled me with awe. I asked the Holy Spirit, "How would my life be different if I truly saw Jesus as leading me flawlessly in every circumstance?" I began to see how vastly better His will is than mine. Exchanging my will for His in any specific situation opens the door to undiscovered continents of experience with God.

The absolute perfection of God's will means every step I take to follow His leadership is a monumental trade up. Every decision, attitude, comment, response, and sacrifice I make to please Him is vastly better for me (and everyone around me) than if I am self-led. In every situation I face today, following His leadership is not a *little* better but *much* better. And the consequences of going my own direction are far worse than I usually imagine.

>> Every decision, attitude, comment, response, and sacrifice I make to please Him is vastly better for me (and everyone around me) than if I am self-led. >>

This is another fork in the road for us. We choose to follow either Jesus or ourselves in each situation we face. The implications of which fork in the road we take are significant.

Honestly, the decisions, attitudes, and comments I most regret came out of occasions when I resisted doing what would please God and chose instead to be self-led. Typically my self-led choices hurt others, created guilt, and caused me to miss the reward I could have enjoyed if I had let Jesus lead me. I think of financial decisions I made on my own and many attitudes at work that created self-inflicted pain such as stress, anger, envy, and worry. This just underscores from personal experience what Jesus says about Himself: He is the only flawless leader. And I am not!

Put another way, each step of following the good Shepherd is a step toward paradise. But trusting our own leadership is a step toward distance from God, self-inflicted injury, and spiritual blindness. Paul used the metaphor of sowing and reaping to describe this truth: *"Do not be deceived, God is not mocked; for whatever a man sows, this he will also reap. For the one who sows to his own flesh will from the flesh reap corruption, but the one who sows to the Spirit will from the Spirit reap eternal life"* (Galatians 6:7-8). One choice sows seeds of vibrant life; the other yields distance from God and a life that is greatly inferior to the one He would have given.

All of us, being children of Adam and Eve, are born with an innate confidence that we can do a pretty good job leading ourselves. But we're born believing a lie, and unless something interrupts the status quo, we'll persist in our self-led lives. But thank God, He is a wonderful disruptor of that kind of life.

THE CONTINUAL LEADER

Those who heard firsthand Jesus' message about the good Shepherd could easily understand His analogy. They knew that a shepherd is devoted to the welfare of animals that aren't capable of properly caring for themselves. They could tell you that a good shepherd provides for, protects, and leads his sheep to nutrition, rest, and safety. He lives his entire life with his sheep; he is always leading them. *"When he puts forth all his own, he goes ahead of them, and the sheep follow him because they know his voice"* (John 10:4).

The phrases "goes ahead of them" and "follow him" use a verb tense that denotes constant action. The shepherd is *continually* leading the sheep, and the sheep are *continually* following.

Similarly, in every situation we face, our good Shepherd is eager to lead us to a place of protection, provision, rest, and nourishment. *Every* situation. It's not that He has an idea or two for us to consider once a week or so. Instead, we wake each morning to a Shepherd who loves leading us throughout the day in every conversation, project, meeting, meal, problem, and issue we face. He *enjoys* walking through life with us. And He always guides us to a monumentally better attitude, comment, decision, or response than we would have arrived at on our own.

>>   In every situation we face, our good Shepherd is eager to lead us to a place of protection, provision, rest, and nourishment. *Every* situation. >>

THE CONTINUAL FOLLOWER

Reflecting on these truths proved bittersweet for me. At first, I was moved that God cares so much about giving me His best. He not only died for me, but He is also continually devoted to helping me live. On the other hand, I grieved over my decisions, attitudes, and actions that have been self-led. Even knowing Him as long as I have, I'm still more self-led than Christ-led in my conversations, decisions, and attitudes. But I am making progress. I seek to please Him in more situations today than I did last year—and that counts with Him. We are all simply children who are called to grow up in Him. Thankfully, His love doesn't vary with our performance.

Remember, not only is the Shepherd's leadership continual in nature, but so is our following of that leadership. We do not follow Jesus in a single grand, sweeping commitment but by one decision, one thought, one comment, and one action at a time.

The most important step we will ever take with Jesus will always be the next one.

Jesus said, *"My sheep hear My voice, and I know them, and they follow Me"* (John 10:27). The two actions mentioned in this verse—hear and follow—describe the essence of the continual following He knows is best for us. As we grow and develop in our walk with Jesus, we will increasingly be able to hear His voice directing us and then do what He leads us to do. Following Jesus is active. It is not passive, and it is far from unconscious. We do not have to wait for a sign from heaven to show up outside our front door to tell us what we should do; we actively and intentionally seek ways that we can please Him in a given situation.

If we were sitting in my living room having coffee and talking over how to do this practically, I would suggest you start with two simple questions. I call them "surrender questions," and they've been incredibly helpful to me in my walk with God. Every time I've shared them with someone I'm mentoring, that person also seems to gain traction in walking with God.

First, I **ask God what to do or say.** Before I interact with my family, friends, or a business colleague, I pray, "Lord, what would You have me do or say?" One morning recently, before having breakfast with Jan, I asked God what I could say to encourage her, knowing that God is the best encourager in the universe. I was quiet for a minute or so, and then an idea popped into my head to encourage her by commending her for the way she helped my daughter with an important decision without being overbearing. I always filter these sorts of impressions through the Word, and this one seemed consistent with what I'd read in Romans 15:5, so I felt confident it was the leading of the Spirit. When I told Jan what I felt the Holy Spirit wanted me to say, tears filled her eyes. She told me she really needed to hear that. She stayed encouraged all that day, and I was elated that God had used me.

At work, I ask God what I can say to team members that would encourage them. It seems as though every time I ask God this question and then say whatever I believe would please Him, the person beams.

I apply this surrender question to other daily choices as well. When I am on the computer or watching television and see something that looks questionable, I ask the Spirit if He is comfortable watching this with me. If there is any doubt, I change channels. Asking what He wants me to do rather than assuming He is okay with all my choices is the difference between being Christ-led and being self-led.

I ask God surrender questions as I read the Scriptures too. For example, a passage I regularly reflect on is, *"Husbands, love your wives, just as Christ also loved the church and gave Himself up for her"* (Ephesians 5:25). I am meant to imitate Jesus' incredible sacrificial love for His children in my love for Jan. So I try to ask this question daily: "Lord, what new sacrifice can I make for Jan to meet her needs and represent Your love for her today?" Another question I frequently ask is, "Lord, where am I falling down in this command?" or "Where have I not honored You?" so I can apologize to her for my shortcomings.

When I am working, I often think of another passage: *"Whatever you do, do your work heartily, as for the Lord rather than for men, knowing that from the Lord you will receive the reward of the inheritance. It is the Lord Christ whom you serve"* (Colossians 3:23-24). I use these verses to shape surrender questions such as, "Lord, how should I do this project differently in light of the fact that I am doing it for You?" or "Lord, what am I doing at work that is *not* pleasing to You?" or "Lord, what could I say to my coworkers to represent You to them?" Your questions will be unique to your specific work situation, but the essence will be the same: "God, what do You want me to do?"

We should never read the Bible as we read the newspaper or a good book, in order to be informed or entertained. The Bible is both informative and entertaining, but it was never intended to be merely those things. It helps us follow Jesus one step at a time by revealing ever more about His Person and His purposes. If I am reflecting on a verse about God's character, I may ask, "Lord, if I really believed this truth, how would You want me to live differently?" Or if I encounter a positive command, such as to love my neighbor, I might ask, "Lord, which neighbor can I love today? How can I express Your love to this person? How have I been cold and indifferent to someone?" This changes my time spent reflecting on the Bible from casual reading to an encounter with the living God.

In the second surrender question, I **ask God what attitude to have.** On any given day, we choose from a range of attitudes. Some of the worst include being critical, selfish, angry, complaining, controlling, demanding, envious, fearful, or self-condemning. Jesus wants to rescue us from these not only because they are wrong in light of His character but also because they are damaging to us and others. They sow deadness in everyone. They rob us of companionship with our God.

Asking God what attitude He would have us adopt in situations is a great way to let Him lead us to a better place. Not long ago, one of my partners sent me an e-mail that really offended me. I set an appointment with him to discuss it and express my anger. But on the morning of the appointment, I asked Jesus what attitude He wanted me to have toward my partner, and I realized my response was wrong. I felt prompted to ask my partner what he meant by the e-mail before I said anything about how it made me feel. I discovered that his intent was completely different from what I understood it to be. God had rescued me from damaging a relationship I genuinely cared about.

Sometimes I will sincerely fight a bad attitude for days. I get some victory over it, and then it pops back up and I have to seek God for His leadership again. I believe this is normal and part of what Paul called *"fight[ing] the good fight of faith"* (1 Timothy 6:12). It is not easy to walk with God when our selfish nature screams at us to do and say what we feel like doing rather than what our Shepherd leads us to do.

When I face a challenging situation, the best thing I can do is ask the Holy Spirit how He would have me respond to the difficulty rather than let my selfish nature run the show. Without His help, I'll react with anger, fear, resentment, or envy. I've found that simply asking the question softens my heart to receive His help.

Not long ago, I was returning from New York late on a Friday afternoon. I was anxious to get home after the long trip, but when I arrived at the airport I discovered the flight was delayed. My nitial response was frustration and complaint. Then, after a few moments of complaining, I asked God what attitude He wanted me to have. Immediately, I started to see my predicament differently. The verse that often comes to mind in situations such as this is, *"Rejoice always; pray without ceasing; in everything give thanks; for this is God's will for you in Christ Jesus"* (1 Thessalonians 5:16-18). I needed to obey the instructions I already knew He'd given. As I began thanking Him for His perfect plan and for the good things He would bring out of the delay, a wave of peace and joy returned. Instead of being miserable, I was able to use the gift of time to catch up on some important projects. In fact, I believe

God was doing something good for everyone on the airplane. He was weaving it into His perfect plan. I eventually settled into my seat on the late flight with gratitude and a chagrined smile at my shortsightedness. When am I going to realize that He always has a better plan than mine? I'm thankful He is patient with me as I continue to learn even after all these years.

Imagine how much richer and more fulfilling our lives could be if we asked these surrender questions several times a day! Letting God lead us to do or say something that pleases Him or to adopt an attitude of trust toward His good plans frees us to follow Him moment by moment.

WHEN HIS DIRECTION IS UNCLEAR

Hearing the Shepherd's voice and following it is a lifelong process. Sometimes when I ask God a surrender question, I don't receive any promptings or impressions. When that happens I do what I believe would please Him according to the Scriptures. At other times, I may get an impression or prompting to do something and later realize it was my voice I heard, not His. Because of this, I qualify any promptings of the Spirit. If I read the Bible and interpret it correctly, then I can say the words, "God spoke to me" just as if I heard an audible voice from heaven. But if I receive an impression from the Spirit about how to apply a verse in a situation, I say instead, "I felt God prompting me to . . ." This distinction is crucial. We have to allow a level of uncertainty with promptings, dreams, or thoughts that come to mind when we pray. On the one hand, such things are vital to walking with God, but on the other, we must stop often and confirm that we're hearing His voice and not our own. This is what it means to walk by the Spirit, and it is so much better than applying principles and commandments at our whim.

Cultivating sensitivity to God's voice is a lifelong process, but with the Holy Spirit as our Helper we don't have to figure any of this out on our own. He is always with us to illumine what God's truth means, to lead us in how to apply the truth, to incline our hearts to follow Him, and to empower us to do what He says. The Bible assures us, *"For all who are being led by the Spirit of God, these are sons of God"* (Romans 8:14).

THE SURRENDERED LIFE

When we become followers of Jesus we surrender our lives to Him. We accept God's leadership in whatever circumstances He brings our way. We hold every dream we have, every relationship, and every possession with a light touch, and we give Him permission to take any of it, knowing He will always give us something better in return plus the strength to endure any loss. We give Him permission to replace our dreams for His, to take away our money to give us the riches of knowing Him better, and to let us experience injustice and persecution. We release our agendas and hold fast to Him. This is the attitude of the surrendered follower.

The opposite attitude is to demand our rights. Our natural selves believe we have the right to be fairly treated, to have what others have, to be respected and appreciated, and to live a pain-free life. So when God gives us a difficult boss, a disease, or a lost sale at work, we get angry because we think God failed to give us what we deserve. But being a follower of Jesus means that life is not about what *we* deserve but about what *He* deserves. This is a fundamental shift in how we view our circumstances that brings so much more joy, peace, and genuine rest than the turmoil of a self-led life.

Giving God what He deserves means we thank Him for His good plan and for the good He will bring about even in loss or difficulty. We humbly affirm His wisdom and acknowledge that He has our best interests at heart.

>> Being a follower of Jesus means that life is not about what we deserve but about what He deserves. This is a fundamental shift in how we view our circumstances that brings so much more joy, peace, and genuine rest than the turmoil of a self-led life. >>

Giving God what He deserves also means we expect great things from God. We are not victims but beneficiaries of His plan. With that mind-set, a man who has lost his job can say to Jesus, "Lord, thank You that I had the job for as long as I did. Thank You for the good things You have planned for me. I adore You for Your perfect wisdom, plans, and motives." When we truly believe that knowing Jesus is the single most important and valuable thing in our lives, then everything else is expendable. Here is how a little-known prophet in the Bible said it:

> *Though the fig tree should not blossom and there be no fruit on the vines, though the yield of the olive should fail and the fields produce no food, though the flock should be cut off from the fold and there be no cattle in the stalls, yet I will exult in the LORD, I will rejoice in the God of my salvation.* (Habakkuk 3:17-18)

We are all probably attracted to the rightness of Habakkuk's attitude. But *adopting* this attitude is often a struggle of our will versus God's will, and our right versus His right to rule and reign over everything. I can't tell you how many times I have said to Him, "Lord, I have a really bad attitude toward You right now. Please help me praise You and thank You. Please loosen my grip on my agenda and help me give You the right to lead me wherever You think is best." Sometimes I struggle with accepting His leadership for minutes, sometimes for hours, and sometimes off and on for a few months. This is all part of fighting the good fight of faith.

>>   It is hell on earth to be angry and bitter at God, to complain that He is unfair or unwise, or to demand that He explain Himself. The only thing worse than a difficult trial is enduring it with a bad attitude toward the God who allowed it for our good and who is devoted to bringing great things from it. >>

Because an attitude of submission to the will of God rises and falls every day, we need to recommit our lives to Him daily as well—to relinquish all rights to our agendas, dreams, or possessions. We must ask Him continually to help us keep a light touch on all we have and desire. We can depend on the Holy Spirit to incline our hearts to accept our circumstances with gratitude and worship. And we must remind ourselves that if we don't give Him permission to lead us, we will be entirely whipsawed by our circumstances and end up stressed, grumpy, nervous, and empty. Part of what makes heaven heaven is that we will be free to yield unreservedly, wholeheartedly, and with reckless abandon to His will and plan. That's the best place we could possibly be.

In contrast, it is hell on earth to be angry and bitter at God, to complain that He is unfair or unwise, or to demand that He explain Himself. The only thing worse than a difficult trial is enduring it with a bad attitude toward the God who allowed it for our good and who is devoted to bringing great things from it.

RESCUE AND RESISTANCE

My life is full of stories of my imperfect efforts to follow Jesus and the extraordinary things He has allowed me to experience at work, at home, or in helping others know and follow Him. I love telling about His loyalty! Yet in spite of my Shepherd's flawless and steadfast leadership, my heart at times resists asking Him what would please Him. On many occasions I've struggled through sleepless nights deciding whether I really believed the things I am now writing about.

One of these struggles occurred when I was twenty. I had dated a girl for four years and wanted to ask her to marry me. Instead, God was clearly leading me to break off the relationship. I argued with Him for a couple of weeks. Meanwhile, all the godly counsel I received confirmed what I already knew in my conscience: Jesus wanted to rescue her from me, and me from her. Finally, I chose to follow God. Three years later He led me to the greatest gift of my life: the girl I married and have loved for thirty-six years. Had I not followed His leadership in this decision, my life would have taken a dramatically different trajectory from the one He had in mind. I can't begin to count the many things I and others would have missed had I made a different decision.

But not every story of following Jesus has seemed to work out well. Sometimes negative consequences have come from *obeying* Him. I have lost friends because I followed His leadership and spoke the truth about their sin. I have had painful things said about my character when I have taught the message in this book. I have faced difficulties at work when I've tried my best to please God.

Jesus' example profoundly inspires me. Even the Son of God struggled to follow God's will wholeheartedly when it meant paying the price for the sins of the world and suffering separation for a period from the Father. The agony of surrender was so great for Jesus that He sweated blood. Yet His prayer just before His arrest reveals a firm devotion to do whatever pleased His Father: *"Father, if You are willing, remove this cup from Me; yet not My will, but Yours be done"* (Luke 22:42). In this single statement, Jesus gave us a model for all of life.

If God left us alone to rely on our determination and discipline to please Him, we'd all give up at the first sign of opposition. But He does at least 99 percent of the work. He shines a light on His flawless nature. He inclines our hearts to follow Him. He empowers us to overcome our stubborn wills so we can enjoy the great reward of pleasing Him. Our part is simply to respond well to His gracious initiation.

British author and speaker Graham Cooke explains this dynamic brilliantly. At Christmas, parents will often give their young children money so they can have the pleasure of buying their parents a gift. All the children must do is receive the money and choose to spend it on their parents rather than themselves. The parents supply the money, drive the kids to the store, help them pay the cashier, and provide the gift-wrapping supplies. Yet the parents are filled with excitement when they open the present. Similarly, as we follow His leadership, God does most of the work and paves the way for our obedience. And then He receives our gifts with joy, especially when following Him demands sacrifice on our parts.

WHY FOLLOW?

I have never met anyone who followed Jesus closely for decades simply because it was the right thing to do. I don't believe people are sustained long-term with that motivation alone.

So why *would* anyone follow Jesus when it often means giving up our agendas, dreams, or desires? God's Word describes three sustainable motivations that, with the help of His Spirit, can push us past the resistance of our selfish will. The first is a holy selfishness that recognizes following Jesus as far and away the best thing we could do with our lives, bearing rewards that will continue for all eternity. This is the simple, backward calculation from the reality that Jesus is the only flawless leader and that everything is vastly better when we follow Him.

The second motivation I see in Scripture is a godly fear of sowing spiritual death by self-led choices. We recognize the danger of a relationship with God that is cold, distant, and nominal. We rightly fear suffering a period of stubborn resistance to His will or even finishing our lives poorly.

But there is another motive that should propel us to trade our ways for His: pleasing God. Who wouldn't want to please a Friend so wonderful, powerful, good, generous, and captivating? When we explore even a portion of His devotion to us, His delight in us, how utterly brilliant He is in everything He does, and how gracious He is with our faults, then making Him happy becomes our greatest joy.

A powerful scene occurs in John's vision of heaven in Revelation 5. He described a vast sea of heavenly creatures that, as they viewed Jesus in all His glory and greatness, were overcome with admiration.

Then I looked, and I heard the voice of many angels around the throne and the living creatures and the elders; and the number of them was myriads of myriads, and thousands of thousands, saying with a loud voice, "Worthy is the Lamb that was slain to receive power and riches and wisdom and might and honor and glory and blessing." (verses 11-12)

As I meditated on this passage recently, I cried out to God, "Forgive me for thinking of You as small and unworthy of leading me. I know You aren't foolish and inconsistent like I am. Open my eyes, Lord, and let me see Your greatness clearly. Please elevate my view of Your worthiness to lead me moment by moment. Forgive me for being so casual about Your leadership!"

What paradise it would be to see God clearly and to be as overcome as the heavenly beings in Revelation with enthusiasm, devotion, and adoration. I know if we could consistently see Him this way, we would *want* to please Him continually, we would be *ambitious* to please Him, and we would *find our joy* in pleasing Him with everything we say, do, and respond to in life.

GREAT REWARD

After my mother's funeral our whole family returned to my parents' house to rest. I went in her bedroom and, to my surprise, found a gift I gave her when I was seven. In second grade, we glued macaroni on cigar boxes and spray-painted the boxes gold to give to our mothers on Mother's Day. My sincere desire to please her with my meager gift so moved her that she used it for more than forty years.

My mother's response was disproportionate to the quality of my gift. And the same is true with God. Every sincere effort to please Him will be rewarded disproportionately by our gracious heavenly Father.

We cannot possibly measure the depth of God's joy when we choose to please Him instead of ourselves in even the smallest way. What may seem meager, even clumsy, to us matters to Him. As a result, every decision, thought, and action we yield to Him will be extravagantly rewarded in heaven beyond our wildest dreams. In this life, too, He will be generous. His greatest gift in this life and the next is *Himself.* Jesus said, *"He who has My commandments and keeps them is the one who loves Me; and he who loves Me will be loved by My Father, and I will love him and will disclose Myself to him"* (John 14:21).

The only way we can truly experience the joy of His unwavering friendship is to follow Him step-by-step, more and more, throughout the course of our lives. The more we do this, the more Jesus will disclose Himself to us. The more we exchange our ways for His best, the more we get to see and know the most wonderful being in the universe. That's always a great exchange.

RESPONDING TO GOD SUGGESTION

Right now, ask Jesus a surrender question about an issue you are facing at work or at home. Think of the issue and ask, "Lord, what would You have me do or say?" or "Lord, how would You have me respond to this person?" Be still for a moment and see what idea comes to mind. If it is consistent with what God has said in the Bible, do it.

Note: For a list of specific surrender questions by area of life, go to www.morethanordinary.org.

CHAPTER NINE

REPRESENTATION

Responding to God's work in the world

When I arrived at the U.S. Air Force Academy in June 1968, the war in Vietnam was raging and so was the antiwar backlash. I was out of sync with most of my generation, but I truly believed God wanted me to enter the service of my country and become a fighter pilot. The year before I had asked God where I should go to college and felt strongly that He wanted me to attend the Academy. I was thrilled to see His hand miraculously clear the way for me to be accepted to the school in the face of stiff competition.

On my first day there, I received my uniform, was given a slew of shots, and got a military haircut. The haircuts set the other cadets and me apart from the rest of our generation, who wore their hair as long as it would grow. The uniform was a tangible reminder of our purpose—to protect and defend our country—and a clear message to the rest of the world that we were willing to die for an effort we believed in. Our superiors continually drove home to us that we represented something bigger than ourselves. They instilled in us traits of honor, courage, and duty. We lived a life of sacrifice and discipline. This held a strong appeal for an idealistic seventeen-year-old who wanted to matter, to do something noble and right, and to make the world a better place.

My fellow cadets and I were not always well received in civilian life. One Saturday night, a classmate went into the nearby downtown area of Colorado Springs wearing his uniform and was beaten nearly to death by some guys our age. When we walked through an airport, it was not uncommon for our peers to approach us and insult us. Not everyone felt this way, but there was enough rage against the war and the military that we encountered animosity most places we went in uniform. Yet opposition only reinforced our sense of purpose.

I can understand the antiwar sentiment of the time. Today, good people still take opposing positions on government policy and the use of the military. But even when holding an opposing view, we can appreciate the rigors of the life of soldiers and the nobility of what most are trying to do. Whenever I see soldiers in the airport I say, "Thanks for serving." And when I see those who have lost a limb or two, I turn away as my eyes fill with tears at their sacrifice.

For nine years I wore my uniform proudly. It was a constant reminder of my purpose and the values I stood for.

REPRESENTING THE KING OF KINGS

As followers of Jesus, we do not represent a single country's way of life or imperfect policies. We represent Someone whose kingdom is greater and nobler than any single country. We represent the King of kings, the Creator of the universe, and the only perfect Person. Knowing and believing that we represent a God this great should transform any day, any task, or any encounter. No higher or more noble purpose exists on the planet than to represent Jesus in daily life, and there is no more effective way to make the world a better place.

>> We represent God and His interests by how we approach our tasks at work and home and by the way we relate to people. We get the honor of joining Him in the good work He is doing. >>

We wake every morning to a King who has significant plans for us that day, specific tasks for us to do that will contribute to His eternal blueprint for human history. He wants to use us as conduits of His love, encouragement, or wisdom to people we meet at work, in the grocery story, in our communities—wherever we are. *We represent God and His interests by how we approach our tasks at work and home and by the way we relate to people. We get the honor of joining Him in the good work He is doing.* Christian mothers and fathers represent Him and His interests and values to their children. A Christian CEO of a company represents Him to all the employees, vendors, and customers. A Christian salesclerk will represent Him to his or her coworkers and customers.

Representing God is not a self-driven pursuit of character

qualities, as though life were a self-improvement course. Representing God is a relationship. It is doing things together *with Him*. We interact with Him, listening to His voice and following His lead. We don't invent our own assignments and do work however we want. Rather, as in the military, we seek direction from our Superior, and we carry out that direction while trusting Him for the strength and ability we need.

Also like soldiers, we who represent God live a life of sacrifice and discipline for the sake of our high calling. This is what Paul meant when he wrote, *"Suffer hardship with me, as a good soldier of Christ Jesus. No soldier in active service entangles himself in the affairs of everyday life, so that he may please the one who enlisted him as a soldier"* (2 Timothy 2:3-4). We're called to a different lifestyle from that of people who live only for themselves in the pursuit of comfort and convenience. But any sacrifices are outweighed by the great honor and privilege of representing God's interests in a world where most live with little or no reference to His presence or authority.

All this makes life an adventure! We never know beforehand how God will use us, and we'll probably have little idea of the fullness of how He did until we get to heaven. But in the meantime, we get to experience the thrill of seeing His power and goodness flow through us to others in any context.

THE FAMILY BUSINESS

If we are going to represent God's interests well, we need to know what they are. We need to understand the family business. Our heavenly Father is by nature a worker, creator, and sustainer who constantly and tirelessly keeps the universe from blowing apart. *"Great are the works of the LORD; they are studied by all who delight in them. Splendid and majestic is His work"* (Psalm 111:2-3).

All day long, God actively and deliberately reveals His goodness and His greatness in every corner of the globe. He masterfully maintains the ecosystem and the natural laws that create air for us to breathe and food for us to eat. His hand sustains every molecule of the universe. On every shore, the ocean stops precisely where He wants it to. There is not one more or less grain of sand on the beach than He desires. He numbers every hair on our heads and knows our days before we live them. Every animal, every tree, every blade of grass is the product of His active work. And all of this devotion to our physical needs and environment is because of His love for us.

The Father who sustains our physical world also cares deeply about our emotional needs. He created family and friends to meet our need to belong in community. And the church is a gift through which God expresses His devotion to meeting our spiritual needs. He is passionate about leading us back to what life was like in the garden, one step at a time.

God is constantly working to meet the physical, spiritual, and emotional needs of humanity. Whenever you see something good, right, just, and loving going on anywhere on the planet, you can know that God is at work. He is ultimately the author, initiator, and motivator of every good thing whether we recognize His role or not. A father loving his son, a woman giving birth to a beloved child, a carpenter building a home, a friend encouraging another, a person deciding to tell the truth—these are all evidence of God's hand at work.

God could accomplish every one of His purposes without our help. But, amazingly, He decided from the beginning to use people as His coworkers. Even after we were exiled from the garden, that didn't change. We can still participate in much of the work He is doing to meet people's needs and can reflect His greatness to a watching world. The good work God planned for each of us to do today was crafted before the beginning of the world. Paul stated in his letter to the Ephesians, *"For we are His workmanship, created in Christ Jesus for good works, which God prepared beforehand so that we would walk in them"* (2:10). Stated even more simply, *"We are God's fellow workers"* (1 Corinthians 3:9).

I don't understand all the reasons a perfect God would use imperfect people like us, but I believe one reason is because of His passion to live life with us and lead us back to paradise. He takes infinite pleasure in letting us partner with Him in His plan for humanity because He loves to share all of life with His children. Working together is one of the key ways God enjoys us and we enjoy Him. (For a fuller discussion of God's view of work and how we can honor Him in it, you may want to read my earlier book *Your Work Matters to God.*)

REPRESENTING THE KING IN OUR WORK

A well-known story tells of a man in London in the Middle Ages watching a church being built. As the construction workers went about their various tasks, he asked a few what they were doing. The first, a stonemason, answered, "I am laying stone with mortar for the wall." Then he asked another stonemason on the other side of the building the same question. His answer was very different: "I am building a great cathedral for God!" What a world of difference between these two answers! I wonder who worked the hardest and who tended to cut corners? I wonder who found joy in work and who found it tedious and boring?

>> We need God to elevate our vision so that we see every task—mowing the yard, doing laundry, paying bills—as working for the King of kings. This transforms and infuses life into even the most boring, frustrating, and difficult jobs we must do. >>

We are all in desperate need of a God-centered vision of work like that of the second stonemason. Too often we think of our daily tasks as secular, which simply means they have no reference to God. This is *vastly* different from seeing ourselves as God's representatives and coworkers. We need God to elevate our vision so that we see every task—mowing the yard, doing laundry, paying bills—as working for the King of kings. This transforms and infuses life into even the most boring, frustrating, and difficult jobs we must do.

One key to this elevated perspective of our daily tasks is found in Ephesians 6. Paul wrote to slaves who had few rights and whose days were filled with menial tasks done for difficult masters. They typically worked long hours every day of the week. Few had vacations or holidays. But the Spirit through Paul said this:

> *Slaves, be obedient to those who are your masters according to the flesh, with fear and trembling, in the sincerity of your heart, as to Christ; not by way of eyeservice, as men-pleasers, but as slaves of Christ, doing the will of God from the heart. With good will render service, as to the Lord, and not to men, knowing that whatever good thing each one does, this*

he will receive back from the Lord, whether slave or free.
(verses 5-8)

From these verses, we can learn a lot that would change our lives, but for now I want to draw your attention to the words *as to Christ*. What does it look like to work as to Christ? It means, I believe, that we take every assignment as a gift from Him, something we can do together with Him. It means we find pleasure in honoring Him with our attitudes and actions. We see Him as our real boss and the only one we must please. It also means we fully trust Him for the results of what we do. Apart from Him we can do nothing. Every good idea or ability comes from Him.

At the same time, doing our work "as to Christ" rather than "as men-pleasers" rescues us from the impossible task of trying to impress people, hoping to be honored by them. The goal of winning the respect and appreciation of people will always lead to disappointment. Only God can give us favor with men. He warns us, *"Stop regarding man, whose breath of life is in his nostrils; for why should he be esteemed?"* (Isaiah 2:22). We can never get self-centered people (as we all are) to honor us in the way we want them to. Even if they do, it will never last long. In contrast, God gives us the incredible privilege of not only pleasing Him in our work but also improving our eternity with rewards for each task we do as to Christ, *"knowing that whatever good thing each one does, this he will receive back from the Lord, whether slave or free"* (Ephesians 6:8). When you think about it, most of our lives are spent on tasks at work or at home. Each task, when done "as to Christ," will receive an eternal reward. I don't know what the rewards will be, but they'll make heaven even better.

Please pause for a moment and consider what this could mean for your life. What if you remembered you were working *with* and *for* God as you completed a few tasks each day over the course of the next week? I believe it would be exciting and life-giving for you. Don't misunderstand; I am not trying to set up a new scoring system for God's approval. I've said it before but it bears repeating: There is no point system for His approval. He already sees you as perfect. His love for you is completely irrespective of your actions. At the same time, He doesn't want you to miss any of the good gifts and experiences He has planned for you. Neither do I!

When we work "as to Christ," we also enjoy greater depth of fellowship with Him. Getting close to a person happens, in part, by building memories of things you did together. To do a task and have a conversation with God during it, asking Him how to please Him, resetting expectations of His presence and power, and having a grateful heart toward Him accomplishes this. I am thankful I have many stories of things Jesus and I have done together. This is one of my favorite things about the adventure of following Him. Many of my memories are of mundane tasks such as mowing the yard or repairing a roof or completing a document. The writing of this book will be one of the tasks I did *with Him* that I will never forget. To see Him give me ideas, use others powerfully to help shape and refine the message, and then have interaction with Him during the writing process is incredibly exciting. It also is wonderful knowing He will get this book into the hands of everyone He wants to read it and will use it perfectly according to His plan.

I try to start my tasks, whether at home or at work, with a prayer that recenters my concept of what I am doing and why I am doing it. If I'm making a sales call I might say, "Lord Jesus, You have called me to serve this person. Thank You for this opportunity. Let me honor You in it. I trust You for the outcome, and I thank You now for what You are going to do even before I see You do it." If I'm starting a project at home, I might pray, "Lord, thank You for the gift of this task. Let me honor You with my attitude and approach and do it together with You." When I am serving the church (my spiritual family), I try to remember I am really serving my Father. When I am gathered with my family or others, I ask Him to show me specific ways I can represent Him well.

Another benefit of working as for Him and connecting with Him in our work is the powerful influence it exerts on others. The fruit of doing our work as to Christ means we are the most enthusiastic, loyal, dedicated, and positive people at work because we're finding significance and joy in what we do. We have a different level of commitment, a higher standard of excellence. We are the most other-centered because we see our coworkers as Jesus does. As a result, most of the people I have known who came to Christ as adults were won through a coworker. Paul told slaves that they must honor God in their work *"so that in every way they will make the teaching about God our Savior attractive"* (Titus 2:10, NIV*).*

Just before I left the Air Force, I stopped to say good-bye to one of the pilots in my squadron who had been particularly critical of my open faith in Jesus. He'd made me the subject of many jokes at the bar on our base and had generally done all he could to make my life difficult. He didn't like the fact that I lived differently from the typical fighter pilot. As I wished him well, he stood, looked me in the eye, and said, "Doug, guys like me need to know that Jesus is real. Please don't stop living whatever way you are living. I need hope that it works for someone. Maybe one day I will follow Jesus too."

I was dumbfounded. You, too, might be surprised by the

people who are watching you to see what life with God looks like. Whether we remember it or not, we are always representing Him. God uses our walk with Him to exert a much more powerful influence on others than we usually realize. Listen to how Paul described our potential influence in a world hostile to God's authority and leadership:

> *Do all things without grumbling or disputing; so that you will prove yourselves to be blameless and innocent, children of God above reproach in the midst of a crooked and perverse generation, among whom you appear as lights in the world, holding fast the word of life.* (Philippians 2:14-16)

NO HIGHER CALL

It makes me sad that many think only pastors and missionaries are God's true representatives. Even the best mission organizations, seminaries, and churches, faced with recruiting and fundraising challenges, tend to misrepresent lasting significance as found only in church or ministry work. In fact, many believers go to seminary and enter the ministry because they think church work is a higher calling than other work. If that were true, then being a lawyer, carpenter, or stay-at-home mom would be second-class duty. That couldn't be further from what the Bible teaches. Yet many accept as truth this deceptive lie. If what we do all day doesn't matter to God, then *we* don't matter to God. I'm happy to say God has a vastly different perspective.

A teacher is not just going to a job; she is representing God in preparing her students for life and reflecting the character of her Father in her attitude and actions. A carpenter is partnering with God to build a home for a family God loves. Grocers feed cities full of people God cares about. Lawyers bring justice to the culture. Doctors bring healing to the sick. Pharmaceutical companies help alleviate pain and suffering and improve the quality of life for people during the years they are on earth.

If you are a waitress, you aren't simply making a living; you are helping people enjoy a meal with the food God has provided. If you are a car salesman, you are doing more than achieving a sales goal; you are helping people travel more safely and efficiently to go to work, take their children to school, and run errands. God ordains all of this work because He is devoted to meeting the needs of His people. When we work in these and other roles, we contribute to things that He as a loving Father wants done. He can—and often does—demonstrate His goodness without our help, but He also loves to show His goodness through what His children do and say.

God doesn't want us to live small lives. One of His greatest gifts is to allow us to partner with Him in His purposes. We are meant to do more than merely survive, make a living, and have a job, a car, and a place to live. We are meant to represent His character to a world desperate to know He is real. We have a high calling and wonderful responsibilities as His children. We are always in uniform, and we represent our King in everything we do.

REPRESENTING GOD TO PEOPLE

Think of your day and all the people you will touch in some manner. Suppose in each situation your question for God was, "Lord, how can I represent Your love for this person?" Of course, we brush by many people and cannot stop to engage everyone.

But the question itself implies a different framework for why we're here. Every interaction is a new opportunity to communicate His love, kindness, and truth in some way, large or small.

God is by nature an encourager, passionate to convey wisdom and eager for fellowship. He takes delight in people and in meeting their needs. When we study the life of Jesus we note that when He saw people, He saw needs. He saw the hungry crowds and miraculously fed them bread and fish. He saw a woman devastated by the loss of her only son, and He raised him from the dead. Jesus wept over crowds who had no spiritual leader and died for us so we could follow Him every day for all eternity. He is without doubt the most thoughtful Person who ever lived.

And we are called to imitate Him: *"Therefore be imitators of God, as beloved children; and walk in love, just as Christ also loved you and gave Himself up for us, an offering and a sacrifice to God as a fragrant aroma"* (Ephesians 5:1-2). We walk in love when we imitate God's love for the world as we go about our daily lives. God will use us in wonderfully spontaneous ways if we will cultivate an awareness of His presence and thoughtfulness of people's needs.

I pulled into a dimly lit, rundown truck stop in Idaho late one night. As I was filling the tank, I tried to shake the mental fog from hours of driving. A big trucker startled me as he walked toward me from out of the shadows. He asked if I wanted to buy any drugs.

I found my mouth moving as though it had a mind of its own. I told him, "I don't want any drugs, but I do have something I would like to give you for free." He was taken aback and asked what I wanted to give him. I said, "I would like to introduce you to the most wonderful Person I have ever known. His name is Jesus. He is crazy about you and wants to give you much more than just money to survive. He wants to forgive you for everything you have done or haven't done that you should have and to invite you to live with Him every day for the rest of eternity. He wants what is best for you now and always. If you will give Him the steering wheel of your life, He will lead you to a much better place. He has transformed my life, and He will yours if you let Him. Would you like to bring Him into your life tonight?" Within minutes, we were both on our knees on the pavement with trucks driving past us as he gave his life to Christ.

I didn't have any trouble staying awake driving after that. I was electrified by how God's Spirit had directed my words and overjoyed that He had used me as a channel of His grace to this man in desperate need of a Savior. I reflected on how clear my words were in spite of my exhaustion and how I'd said things I had never said before. That night I partnered with my heavenly Father, and I knew I wanted to spend the rest of my life living this way. It is an honor to represent Him to others.

Any of us can be used by God to encourage a store clerk, to pray for people we pass on the sidewalk, or to represent Him well to coworkers. He will also give us opportunities to tell people how amazing Jesus is. When we're walking with God we can't help but overflow with Him. If we ask Him for opportunities to share Him with others, He'll provide them.

So if God calls His children to represent His thoughtfulness, patience, and devotion to meeting others' needs, then why in the world are so many followers of Jesus living such unremarkable lives?

One of the greatest contradictions occurs in how we as Christians represent God in our marriages. It is a well-known and heartbreaking fact that Christians have a slightly *higher* divorce rate than the general population.[1] Why would children of God who are themselves experiencing the most amazing grace be unable to express that same grace to their mates? Why would objects of His infinite loyalty and patience break their vows to God and each other? Why would children of a Father devoted to truth believe such lies about how life works? Worse, why would many marriages among believers who will never divorce fall so short of what could be between two people who have the Spirit of life within them? I believe the reason is that few of us have ever learned how to conduct our marriages with God leading our words, attitudes, and actions.

However, I've also heard another, lesser-known statistic that the divorce rate among couples who pray together daily is 1 in 39,000![2] Now, that makes sense to me. I don't believe these couples stay together because they mechanically recite a prayer or read a few verses together. I think these are results of a deep and rich relationship with God that drives them to want to please Him in their marriage. God leads them in how they speak to their spouses and how they represent God's heart to them. They seek to have a God-centered marriage every day. With God's help, they are learning to die to their own needs and desires so they can be attentive, devoted, and determined to love the other no matter what. They are thoughtful, loyal, grace-filled, patient people because of God's enabling. They reflect the best Encourager in the universe to their spouses. When they fail each other, as they often will, they are quick to apologize with heartfelt sorrow.

We are called to represent our God and do His work in the world in our marriages, our jobs, our families, our church, and the larger society. It is the highest purpose on earth. But we were never meant to do it alone. We are called to do life *with God*— relating to Him, led by Him, and enjoying His friendship. As we choose to represent God in increasing dimension and depth, we will know Him increasingly well and enjoy Him more fully. Make no mistake; we will have to battle against our selfish nature. But it is a battle we can win with His help.

BECOMING CHANNELS OF HIS GOODNESS

My natural-born instinct is to believe that the more I focus on me, the happier I will be. Human nature exerts a strong pull in this direction. Americans are taught to dream of retirement when we can enjoy whatever riches we've saved and do exactly what we want every day of our lives. This is made to seem like heaven. But selfishness does not bring life. The American dream doesn't equal joy. It usually doesn't even lead to long-term happiness. We were created with our heavenly Father's DNA to devote ourselves to meet the needs of people He brings to our path in the course of everyday life.

Followers of Jesus invest themselves heavily to help people. They live lives of sacrifice and discipline for the reward of seeing people enjoy walking with Jesus all their days. My friends Mark and Sherri Bankord founded a remarkable church in Rockford, Illinois. My partner, Clyde Jackson, has started ministries around the world while maintaining his business. Frank and Cathy Tanana of Detroit, Michigan, have invested themselves for more than twenty years in helping men and women grow deeper in following Jesus—both during the time Frank was a major-league pitcher and following his retirement. The list of such friends goes on, and I am so proud of them. Some have been foster parents, some have founded schools or hospitals, and some have contributed other significant but less noticeable service for the

King. But all of them would say they get more out of serving than they give.

>> Followers of Jesus invest themselves heavily to help people. They live lives of sacrifice and discipline for the reward of seeing people enjoy walking with Jesus all their days. >>

Some days I lose perspective on what I am doing and why, and I slump into survival mode. But God constantly reminds me of my high calling to serve Him, to represent His words and His attitudes, and to be His hands in every arena of life. This is another part of the journey with Him in which progress, not perfection, is the goal this side of heaven. But God, as always, is disproportionately generous in His rewards for even our most meager efforts.

And if you give yourself to the hungry
And satisfy the desire of the afflicted,
Then your light will rise in darkness
And your gloom will become like midday.
And the LORD will continually guide you,
And satisfy your desire in scorched places,
And give strength to your bones;
And you will be like a watered garden,
And like a spring of water whose waters do not fail.
Those from among you will rebuild the ancient ruins;
You will raise up the age-old foundations;
And you will be called the repairer of the breach,
The restorer of the streets in which to dwell. (Isaiah 58:10-12)

Life is counterintuitive. The more we represent God by choosing to see and meet the needs of people, the happier we will be. The more we show the world who the Father is, the more significant our lives will become. And the more we channel His goodness, the closer we will be to Him.

RESPONDING TO GOD SUGGESTIONS

Right before launching into any task today, pause and ask God how you could do that task in a way that would please Him. Be quiet for a moment and see what comes to mind. It could be that you would do the task differently, you might have a different attitude about it, or you might want to talk to Him while doing it. See how that changes the way you enjoy Him in the midst of the task.

Consider the person closest to you. It could be a spouse, child, parent, or friend. Ask God how you could better represent His love, encouragement, kindness, and sacrificial loyalty to that person today. What would you say or do differently?

Note: For a list of some ideas on how to represent Him to the people around you in a task at work or at home, go to www.morethanordinary.org.

COMING HOME

Responding to a God who loves fresh starts

One summer afternoon my oldest son, Jason, came into the kitchen to talk. His expression was unusually serious. Clearly, something was very wrong. Jan and I sat with our stomachs in our throats and listened to Jason for what seemed like hours. It was worse than we thought.

In the emotional fog, a few things stood out. Jason was worried about his brother, Matt, who was about sixteen at the time and mixed up in something destructive. Jan and I were dazed at first but soon felt the stabbing pain of reality. We felt like failures as parents, each of us wondering what *we* did to cause him to do these things. We felt enormous grief over the trajectory of his life and the pain ahead for him. I was shocked by the irony that I had written books distributed around the world and spoken before thousands about pleasing God only to discover I was unable to help my own son whom I loved more deeply than all the large crowds combined. We were devastated, embarrassed, and heartbroken for our child.

After we composed ourselves, we sat down with Matt and asked if the reports of his behavior were true. Matt showed no remorse or shame. Instead, he lashed out about how his actions were none of our business. We watched with horror as a seemingly insurmountable relational wall was built before our eyes.

As much as I love my two other kids, for the next several weeks most of my thought and prayer was directed toward Matt. Yet Jan and I saw no improvement. Our conversations were getting nowhere. He reacted angrily when we spoke to him on any subject. Still, Jan and I knew we could never stop pursuing Matt until our relationship was restored.

After praying about it, I decided to take him on a scuba trip. That may seem an odd thing to do at such a time, but my strategy was simply to love Matt unconditionally and represent God's kindness, loyalty, and faithfulness to him. Neither of us was certified, so we spent several weekends together training in a pool before the trip. This forced us to talk about our equipment, to test each other before the written exam, and to practice techniques together. During our training, the ice melted slightly, but most of the relational distance remained.

Once we arrived in the Caribbean, we did two or three dives a day, ate meals together, and interacted far away from his buddies. I wanted Matt to feel my love, my delight in being with him, and my relentless devotion to what is best for him. I did not bring up his struggles on the trip. Instead I got him to laugh and to share stories about the dives and what he saw underwater.

On the last day of our trip, his attitude began changing. He talked a little more, smiled a little more, and was even willing to pray before our meal.

Over the next couple of months, Matt slowly returned to the Lord and to us. The highlight came when he sat down and admitted that what he did was wrong and apologized for the pain he'd created. I was so proud of him. It felt as though a forty-ton weight was lifted from my shoulders. We had gotten our son back!

Today Matt is a great man of God who has influenced many lives. He is a loving husband and father and is passionate about talking with God and interceding for others.

CYCLES AND YOYOS

Even in the healthiest of homes, kids and parents experience cycles in their relationship. Wills collide, but such collisions are usually followed by a genuine desire to be close to one another again. God made us to have a deep desire for our parents' affection, attention, and devotion. We are created to be delighted in, to be enjoyed, and to be the apple of our father's eye. Even though my dad has passed away, I still feel a deep longing for these things. We also long for the nurturing affection, attention, and loyalty of a mother and the safety her love provides. But human nature gets in the way of enjoying life with parents at times.

Sometimes my kids when they were young would go off and pout, silently punishing Jan and me for giving them a rule they did not agree with. They questioned our motives at times, accusing us of selfishness because we did not do what they wanted. But other times, they couldn't wait for me to come home so they could show me a new dance routine or how well they could throw the football or because they simply wanted to talk.

All parents need to prepare themselves for these erratic relational cycles. Children will misread our good motives and misunderstand the depth of the wisdom we've gained through hard-won experience. They won't always appreciate the breadth of our devotion for them. Children mature slowly and almost never in a seamless progression. A parent's job is to love children through the process of growing up with the humility that comes from remembering that we were no different or better with our parents. We went against their counsel, kept them awake at nights, and probably horrified them with some of the decisions we made.

It's also crucial to keep in mind that a child's erratic loyalty toward a parent is a lot like ours with our heavenly Father. I may have just turned sixty, but more than ever before I remain a *child* of God. And that means, at times, I am still childish. Every day of my life, my love and loyalty for my heavenly Father yoyos and my heart vacillates.

Sometimes I respond well in a circumstance by enjoying God's presence, seeing His hand, conversing with Him, pleasing Him, expecting Him to fulfill His promises toward me, and representing Him well to others. I can be grateful, celebrating His goodness to me and adoring Him for His power, wisdom, or affection. At times my heart truly echoes David's exuberant proclamation, *"I have set the LORD continually before me; because He is at my right hand, I will not be shaken. Therefore my heart is glad and my glory rejoices; my flesh also will dwell securely"* (Psalm 16:8-9). These are my best hours on the planet—deeply satisfying whether I am actively working or quietly reflecting, whether my circumstances are easy or hard.

But in the blink of an eye, I can cycle in the opposite direction. I respond in subtle independence, deliberate rebellion, or anywhere in between. I ignore God, choose my own counsel, and do what I want when I want to do it. I complain and think destructive thoughts. I can spend an hour, a morning, or even a large portion of the day with little or no thought of Him. Instead of being caught up in enjoying God I am consumed with my circumstances. During these times, my heart is cold and indifferent to His presence and personality. I am self-reliant and self-willed, and I seek the attention of others for the sake of my own ego rather than God's glory.

>> It's crucial to keep in mind that a child's erratic loyalty toward a parent is a lot like ours with our heavenly Father. >>

During difficult or frustrating circumstances, I often arrogantly sit in judgment of God's wisdom or leadership before I realize what I'm doing. I think of Him as cruel, indifferent, unwise, or unfair. I start believing He might not have my best interests at heart. I would never say these things out loud, but I sure think them. Often my desires—what I want to accomplish, how I want a situation to turn out, or how I want people to respond to me—harden into the belief that such things are my *right*. Then I get angry with God for not serving me properly as if He were a waiter at a restaurant getting my order wrong. When He does not give me what I think I deserve, I complain instead of being thankful. These hours are the worst of my life. They reveal that I still have a lot of growing up to do.

We all fail at times to follow His leadership. We all go our own ways for a moment, an hour, or several days. What we do next after we've behaved like foolish children is vital to our walk with Him.

WHAT SIN IS AND WHAT IT ISN'T

Most of the time, when God's children walk away from the Father toward a direction of their own choosing, sin is at work.

Can we be honest? Sin is embarrassing and uncomfortable to talk about. It takes courage, humility, and a sincere desire to please God to even broach the subject. Like a relative of ours who didn't want to go to the doctor to be checked for a reoccurrence of cancer because she was afraid of bad results, so we often avoid spiritual reality checks. We would rather pretend everything is fine.

One reason we don't like to talk about sin is because we have a general fogginess about what it is. If you ask most people to define sin, they would describe behavior such as adultery, lying, stealing, and murder. That list allows most law-abiding citizens to feel pretty good about their lives. But the truth is, sin is much broader and deeper than a list of prohibitions.

Sin is an inner thought, a dishonoring attitude, or a deliberate action that grieves and offends God. Sin can be subtle—halfhearted response to God's Word, for example—or an outright rejection of His commands and instructions. Sin distorts the truth about God and how life works. It entices us with cheap counterfeits while keeping us from the good things God wants to give us. Most of our sin is not what we do but indifference to His presence and leadership. It is not so much about our actions as about what is in our hearts and minds.

Sin causes hurt and offense to a Person who loves us deeply and is crazy about us. It is *always* personal, and it *always* creates relational distance—between God and us, and often between us and other people who are injured by our sin. There is no such thing as a private sin.

God hates sin's destructiveness, but that doesn't mean He hates us. In fact, His hatred of sin only makes Him more passionate about rescuing us from it. God knows that sin is what is killing us. He knows it ruins lives, destroys legacies, and robs people of closeness to Him. He knows that our return to Him when we sin, while hard to think about, is a vital part of experiencing the full life He has in mind for us. When we step away from God, we have to learn to recognize what we've done and correct our direction quickly. Otherwise, we'll only keep getting further away from Him. And I'm sorry to say that we'll have to correct our course often until we get to heaven. This is a major part of what makes heaven such paradise. On earth, the goal can only be progress—often three steps forward and two steps back every day. Perfection comes in heaven. Meanwhile, God is kind enough not to pull back the curtain and let us see all of our sinful selfishness, pride, and unbelief at once. He shows us only enough to keep us walking in the right direction—toward Him.

>> God hates sin's destructiveness, but that doesn't mean He hates us. In fact, His hatred of sin only makes Him more passionate about rescuing us from it. >>

Knowing what sin *isn't* may be as important as knowing what sin is. It is crucial, for example, not to mistake immaturity for sin. Every day I do things that are clumsy and foolish because I still have growing up to do. I have made many decisions fully convinced that I was doing what God wanted, only to find out later that was not the case. My heart was sincere, but I lacked knowledge and maturity that would allow me to do the godliest thing at the moment. This is all part of growing up as children of God.

Every child needs a chance to learn things that only experience can teach. When I was ten, I decided to help my parents by weeding the flowerbeds. I couldn't wait to show my mother the results of my hard work, but there was a small glitch. I had unwittingly pulled up all her carefully planted flowers. What I did that day wasn't rebellion; I just didn't know any better.

Today I am more mature in my walk with God—and my knowledge of landscaping—but I still make many mistakes. While earthly parents may lose patience with their children's lack of maturity from time to time, God doesn't feel the same way. His patience is beyond our comprehension.

It also isn't sin to struggle to trust God in the midst of difficult circumstances. During trials, having a good attitude and response to Jesus can be much harder; this is part of being called to fight the good fight. Finding our joy in Him when surrounded by enemies, disasters, and conflicts truly is a battle. But far from being sinful to struggle, it is holy and right to fight against fleshly desires, the groupthink of the world, and the lies of the Devil. Don't feel you are failing when walking with God is not easy! If you are fighting hard to do His will when everything in you is screaming "No!" then you are winning. Keep fighting, knowing God will give you all the strength you need for the battle.

For all kinds of reasons, we constantly cycle toward and away from God every day. The key is to identify when we've wandered by following a sinful attitude or action and then to return home quickly.

HOW GOD SEES THE WANDERER

Jesus understood that without a clear grasp of the Father who waits for our return, we would keep wandering, too proud, too ashamed of what we've done, or too afraid of what might await us at home. He wanted to remove from our minds and hearts any shadow of doubt about God's passion for restoring His children, so He told three surprising stories, which are recorded in Luke 15.

The first story is of a shepherd relentlessly pursuing a lost sheep and carrying the sheep home with celebration. Jesus told the crowd, including many who hated to admit they were sinners, *"In the same way, there will be more joy in heaven over one sinner who repents than over ninety-nine righteous persons who need no repentance"* (verse 7).

The second story describes a woman who searches for a lost coin that represents her entire life savings. Upon finding it, she calls her friends and neighbors to celebrate (see verse 9). Are you sensing a theme here? These parables give us great insight into God's passion to help us return to Him when we get lost.

The climax of Luke 15 is a story about a father with two sons. We're going to focus on the wayward son who wants to live life on his terms. He believes all he desires can be better obtained without his pesky family, especially his father, looking over his shoulder. He's convinced that a little freedom and independence will make him truly happy. So he casually asks his dad for his portion of the estate and moves on to more exciting pastures.

The son is a picture of the worst parts of us, isn't he? As a father, I read this and want to shout, "Don't you know what you are walking away from? Don't you know you are leaving a place where you're loved for a place that can only corrupt you?" But I am indicted by my own questions when I consider how I treat my

Father. I am constantly wandering from Him.

The father loves his son way too much to force him to stay. He lets the young man choose life on his own terms even though it hurts the father more than he can say. Our heavenly Father also never forces us to respond well to Him or to accept His best. He will not shove paradise with Him down our throat. He won't make us be loyal to Him. He lets us have as much joy in His presence as we choose to have. As Bible teacher Dr. John Oswald Sanders once said, "You will be as close to Him not as you wish to be or hope to be, but as you *choose* to be."[1]

Jesus explained what the son did with his freedom: *"And not many days later, the younger son gathered everything together and went on a journey into a distant country, and there he squandered his estate with loose living"* (verse 13). The story does not say how the father felt about his son's departure, but it isn't hard to imagine. Neither is it hard to imagine how God feels when we wander and squander the wealth He gives us in Christ. While it is true that God is the happiest Person in the universe, when we wander from Him He still grieves with the sadness of a Father completely devoted to our best, fully passionate for fellowship with us, and always wanting to protect and provide for us.

After the money was gone, the young man in Jesus' story had a revelation. Jesus says that *"he came to his senses."* His independence hadn't yielded the results he expected. He was hungry and alone, and he asked himself, *"How many of my father's hired men have more than enough bread, but I am dying here with hunger!"* (verse 17).

I am stuck by the powerful words "when he came to his senses." There is a point in every day when I have said something, done something, or just ignored God and I suddenly sense the loss. I wake up as though from a sleep and ask myself, *What have I done?* I believe this is a common experience for those who walk with

God, and it is a good experience. The worse thing is not to notice!

Having come to his senses, the younger brother in Jesus' story came up with a plan. He rehearsed it in his head—maybe many times—to be sure he'd be ready. He knew he'd have only one chance to rescue his life, if his dad even gave him that much. He said to himself, *"I will get up and go to my father, and will say to him, 'Father, I have sinned against heaven, and in your sight; I am no longer worthy to be called your son; make me as one of your hired men'"* (verses 18-19).

Coming to our senses is a holy moment, but so is admitting what we did was wrong and returning to God for forgiveness. This is a fundamental part of walking with God—coming to Him with no excuses, no justification, and in full awareness that we are unworthy of forgiveness, yet still trusting His goodness. We see all of this in the wandering son's sincere desire simply to return home to his father, on any terms.

The father in Jesus' story is portrayed as watching on the horizon for his son to return. I'm deeply moved by this picture of God longing for my return, eager to welcome me home and give me undeserved kindness. I find it beyond comprehension. Jesus describes it this way: *"But while he was still a long way off, his father saw him and felt compassion for him, and ran and embraced him and kissed him. And the son said to him, 'Father, I have sinned against heaven and in your sight; I am no longer worthy to be called your son'"* (verses 20-21).

In the exuberance of his welcome, the father interrupted his son's apology before the son even got to the part about becoming a hired hand. What nonsense to think the father would let his son be a slave in his household anyway. Instead, the father started planning the welcome-home party. *"But the father said to his slaves, 'Quickly bring out the best robe and put it on him, and put a*

ring on his hand and sandals on his feet; and bring the fattened calf,
kill it, and let us eat and celebrate; for this son of mine was dead and
has come to life again; he was lost and has been found.' And they
began to celebrate" (verses 22-24).

As with many of the most captivating stories, it's the twist
that gets us. We expect the father to be so disgusted with his
son's poor choices that he'd never want to see him again. We
expect righteous anger and maybe even retribution for the way
the son had insulted the father. But what happened? Despite
everything the son had done, the father loved him and wanted
him home. Not just that, he wanted to celebrate his son who
had been lost but was now found. The contrast between the
decadence and loneliness of the son's lifestyle when he was on
his own and the truly satisfying celebration when he came home
is palpable. Fellowship with his sons was the father's highest
value.

>> God is always eager to give us a fresh
   start. >>

Jesus told these three stories to give us a window into the
heart of God. The first story shows us the joy of a shepherd with
the return of his sheep and reveals a God who loves and cele-
brates fresh starts. The second story of the lost coin points out
our great value to Him. And the third story reveals the nature of
God's Father-love toward His wandering children. Our heavenly
Father *never* gives up on us, *never* walks away in disgust, and
never stops having compassion for our pain (even when we've
brought it on ourselves). He sometimes allows us to suffer the
natural consequences of poor decisions for our ultimate good. In
fact, I believe much of our pain is self-inflicted. What I mean is

that much of the stress, insecurity, fear, boredom, and shame we feel is a result of moving away from the Father and His leadership. Even so, God's sons and daughters will not be condemned or shamed for their foolishness and rebellion. Our mistakes don't take Him by surprise. "He is never disillusioned as He has no illusions in the first place," said British author and speaker Graham Cooke.[2]

So we find a stunning set of truths here. First, we are constantly wandering off, like children do with their parents. Love and loyalty cycle with complaint, resistance, pouting, deception, and rebellion. But God is always eager to give us a fresh start. The depth of joy He experiences when we confess our sin to Him is seen clearly in the extravagant celebration the father held for his prodigal son and the honor of a robe and ring. Why would we not want to be restored to relationship with a Father like that? The reception He gives us accounts for the word *therefore* in one of my favorite verses: *"Therefore repent and return, so that your sins may be wiped away, in order that times of refreshing may come from the presence of the Lord"* (Acts 3:19).

HOW TO RETURN

All of us who wander can take heart in this simple, incredible truth: *"There is now no condemnation for those who are in Christ Jesus"* (Romans 8:1). No sin that we as His children commit will make Him reject us or be anything but eager to have us return. Whether it is a moment of independence or a season, God will never condemn us or leave us in disgust. Don't get me wrong. Our sin *does* matter. Our relationship with God will need to be restored often through confession and apology. But God's love and acceptance of His children never wavers through it all. We don't ever have to feel insecure about His love no matter what. He is *never* passive-aggressive or sullen. He will never tire of giving us new chances. We will always find Him friendly and eager to give us a fresh start—even many times a day.

With those truths about God firmly in mind, we can bring our failures to Him in assurance of a loving welcome and then take the next step: confession. Confession means we acknowledge to our Father which attitudes, actions, or words were wrong. We admit without excuse that our behavior was offensive to God, and we bring Him a broken spirit that is eager to change. True confession comes from the heart because that's where God looks, and it includes devotion on our part not to repeat the offense.

After we restore our love for God and renew our fellowship with Him through confession—that is, agreeing with God about our sin—then we need to move forward with the confidence that God offers us a fresh start. The Bible assures us, *"If we confess our sins, He is faithful and righteous to forgive us our sins and to cleanse us from all unrighteousness"* (1 John 1:9). The cleansing God gives us through confession lets us put our sin behind us and look forward to walking with Him even more closely. We also need to forgive ourselves as He has forgiven us. Part of following Jesus is seeing ourselves the way He sees us.

Over the years, I have noticed *two extremes to avoid* when we respond to God about our sin. The first, and the most common, I believe, is to be casual about sin. I have known many professed followers of Jesus—even church leaders—who do not see actions such as complaining, deception, or harsh words as unambiguously wrong: offensive to God, injurious to us, and damaging to others. They excuse anger or gossip, for example, as personality traits rather than habitual sins.

Another way of being casual about sin is to give up trying to please God. We usually do this because we believe following God's commands is a losing battle. Besides, we reason, we can count on His forgiveness. This nonchalance fails to comprehend the relational distance that unconfessed sin creates. It also questions God's authority and goodness. God's commands are always for our good. They weren't given merely to inform us of what is right or as unattainable ideals. They are meant to lead us to a different, fuller life. To be casual about sin or about God's authority is to wander from His presence more than we know.

Others seem to grade themselves on a curve. They try to justify themselves with the argument that they aren't as bad as someone else they know. Instead of asking God to evaluate their hearts, they invent their own measuring stick for life. But God is serious about sin. He doesn't negotiate. We read in Proverbs, *"The fear of the LORD is to hate evil; pride and arrogance and the evil way and the perverted mouth, I hate"* (8:13).

To love one thing requires hating everything that gets in the way of what we love. To love my wife means I hate adultery. The more we value friendship with God, the more we hate sin. We must regularly confess our mistakes to God without excuse and redouble our efforts to respond to Him differently. There is no room for nonchalance; the price is too high.

Our postmodern culture makes it easy to be casual about sin. But another harmful extreme lies at the other end of the spectrum. That extreme rightly takes sin seriously but responds poorly thereafter. People who fall victim to this error feel so much shame about failure that they cannot enjoy the Father. They feel worthless. They listen to the whispers of the Evil One, who tells them they'll never be good enough and cannot move forward because of the past. My history makes me especially vulnerable to this trap. I remember all too well what it was like to sit on a fence in the cold, feeling unwanted and worthless.

It is right and healthy to ask God to expose wrong attitudes you have toward your boss, spouse, coworkers, or friends. You can ask Him to expose ways you love other things more than Him or how you have ignored His leadership or the habits or attitudes you have that are displeasing. When you read a command in your Bible, you can ask God when you may have offended Him by not following it, and He will tell you if you have. It will be a specific event at a specific time, and it will lead you to confession and complete cleansing. If, after this kind of search, you struggle with a general sense of condemnation and worthlessness not attached to a specific command or situation, that feeling is *not* from God but from the Devil.

We are right to feel sorrow when we offend God and act in a way that is not worthy of Him. We are also right to come to Him knowing we don't deserve to be taken back but confident He will always welcome us with eager arms. But we must not hate ourselves, consider ourselves worms, or feel worthless. That would be to see ourselves differently than God sees us. Self-hatred is a counterfeit of humility; it looks a lot like it from the outside but has none of the fruits of the real thing. Paul explained it like this: *"For the sorrow that is according to the will of God produces a repentance without regret, leading to salvation, but the sorrow of the world produces death"* (2 Corinthians 7:10).

The "sorrow of the world" is narcissistic. It is rooted in pride and self-pity, both of which make us reluctant to return humbly to God. Jesus spoke to this with words that have helped me enormously in fighting my tendency toward shame and feelings of worthlessness when I have failed God: *"No one, after putting his hand to the plow and looking back, is fit for the kingdom of God"*

(Luke 9:62). No one can drive well while looking in the rearview mirror. God wants my eyes forward, on where He is leading me next, not backward from where I've wandered.

ALWAYS RETURNING

We all have a lot in common with the prodigal, which is a humbling realization. The best of us cycle through a day turning to God and then turning away from Him. But we must view confessing our sin as a step forward on the journey, because that's how God views it. In fact, because of our sin nature, constantly returning to Him is a great victory. The worst thing we could do is keep going in a self-directed lifestyle—suffering greater distance from God, blindness to how life works, and much self-inflicted pain.

>> The best of us cycle through a day turning to God and then turning away from Him. But we must view confessing our sin as a step forward on the journey, because that's how God views it. >>

God's passion to give us a fresh start is worth celebrating, as one Puritan writer was wise enough to see in this prayer titled "Continual Repentance":

I am always standing clothed in filthy garments,
And by grace am always receiving change of raiment,
For thou dost always justify the ungodly;
I am always going into the far country,
And always returning home as a prodigal,

Always saying, Father, forgive me,
And thou art always bringing forth
The best robe.
Every morning let me wear it,
Every evening return in it,
Go out to the day's work in it,
Be married in it,
Be wound in death in it,
Stand before the great white throne in it,
Enter heaven in it shining as the sun.
Grant me never to lose sight of
The exceeding sinfulness of sin,
The exceeding righteousness of salvation,
The exceeding glory of Christ,
The exceeding beauty of holiness,
The exceeding wonder of grace.[3]

My prayer for you is that you'll learn to love God more deeply every day. I want you to enjoy life with Him more and more with each passing month. One essential, nonnegotiable part of that is diligently asking God to cleanse you of attitudes, thoughts, and actions that rob you of the joy of His presence. The more often you return to Him when you've wandered, the more at home in His presence you'll feel. And it is a very good thing to feel at home where you actually belong—with Him.

RESPONDING TO GOD SUGGESTIONS

Take a quiet moment to ask God if you had any attitude, word, or action today that was offensive to Him. Sit quietly and see what comes to mind. If nothing specific comes to mind, move on. If something specific comes to mind, confess it to Him and thank Him for forgiveness. Press on to know and follow Him.

Think of the thing in your life you are most ashamed of. If you haven't confessed it, then do so. But if it is a lingering sense of shame long after you have been forgiven, thank God that He will never fail or forsake you, never leave in disgust, and never condemn you. See yourself as He does in this case—as though you never did it. Move on.

UNTIL PARADISE

Responding to God for a lifetime

You're in good company if you feel a little overwhelmed at this point. You've encountered a lot of big ideas in these pages, but take heart. Cultivating a lifestyle of enjoying God is a fascinating pursuit for a lifetime, not something you nail down in five easy but shallow steps.

I've described a number of practices that make life with God an adventure. Please don't try to start all of them simultaneously and immediately. I suggest that you go back through the book and identify one way you'd like to respond to God right now and then take some time to work on making it a part of your life. Better yet, ask God which idea *He* would like you to start with and then do what you think would please Him. Above all, remember that the goal is not a new spiritual to-do list; the goal is to respond to God a little more each day. So whatever you choose to do next, let it be in response to His love for you and His delight in your companionship instead of an attempt to work hard enough to be worthy of His presence.

>>   The goal is not a new spiritual to-do list; the goal is to respond to God a little more each day. >>

I write out of a deep concern for your generation. I worry about the traps and distractions the Evil One has set to rob you of the extraordinary life God planned for you. And I worry about the kind of spirituality my generation has modeled for you. To look at most of us, you'd conclude that our experience with God is boring, passive, shallow, and hard work even if it began with joy, passion, and freedom. We have shown you a life with God that is primarily about living in the seen world and being whipsawed by life's ups and downs. Many of my generation (and some of yours, too) suffer a stale, stoical, or legalistic relationship with God yet think of themselves as doing well spiritually. Tragically, they don't know what they are missing.

With those concerns driving me, I've written with a passion to help you live full to the brim with Jesus. I want so much more for you than only a vague familiarity with the life God promises His children. I know I have fulfilled this mission clumsily in many ways, and I still struggle to walk with Him fully myself. But looking back, I can see that all the other books I wrote were merely precursors to this life message.

THE BEST OUTCOME

I hope that when you think of your heavenly Father, you see Him as majestic, generous, and fully delighting in you. I want you to enjoy an ever-expanding view of God throughout the course of your life, to think big thoughts of Him every day, and to see more and more flashes of His power and love for you in your circumstances. God is a perfect Father whose intention has always been to help you have the kind of life Adam and Eve had before the fall: paradise. I hope you are captivated by this God, arrested by His generosity, and consumed with knowing and following Him every day as you walk toward this paradise.

I hope you will enter into a deeper conversation with your God. I like to imagine you processing all of life with Him. This kind of conversation will rescue you from concepts of life with God that are not biblical. I hope you'll discover that connection with God has very little to do with an inanimate list of rules, and everything to do with interacting with a Person who is always present and interested in everything you do. I hope you'll even use this book to enrich that conversation as you listen for what He is saying to you through its pages.

I hope that knowing God will transform your entire approach to daily life. I hope you'll make your goal a moment-by-moment connection with Him in the full range of life's responsibilities. I hope you'll never again imagine Him as distant. He has planned every part of your day so that you can experience it with Him. And His plans are infinitely better than what you've come up with. They lead you to the best life possible.

I hope a better picture of God will help you see the rest of the world differently. I hope that everything you do acquires meaning and significance. I hope you'll see God as towering over each circumstance and problem you face, which will relieve you of a lot of unnecessary stress, fear, and difficulty. Knowing life isn't up to you makes everything easier.

I hope this book will simplify the way you walk with God. In any relationship, you need to do only a few things well to have a healthy and growing connection. In a relationship with God, the spiritual disciplines are helpful as a means to the end of seeing and responding to God, but they are not ends in themselves. If you make them the end, you'll be overwhelmed. Instead, I hope that your time in the Word, in prayer, in church, in all your spiritual practices will boil down to this simple focus: to encounter an amazing God and to respond to Him.

I hope you will pass on what you've learned. We are made to reproduce. God created us that way. I am convinced that if we don't become spiritual parents and brothers and sisters to others—helping them experience a walk with God that is more than ordinary—we will not walk with God over the long haul. Please don't miss the legacy God wants you to leave.

All of my hope could be captured in this statement: **I want you to experience more and more paradise until you have it in full.** This is God's hope for you too. Here's a great summary.

> *So here's what I want you to do, God helping you: Take your everyday, ordinary life—your sleeping, eating, going-to-work, and walking-around life—and place it before God as an offering. Embracing what God does for you is the best thing you can do for him. Don't become so well-adjusted to your culture that you fit into it without even thinking. Instead, fix your attention on God. You'll be changed from*

the inside out. Readily recognize what he wants from you, and quickly respond to it. Unlike the culture around you, always dragging you down to its level of immaturity, God brings the best out of you, develops well-formed maturity in you. (Romans 12:1-2, MSG)

LIVING IN COMMUNITY

I hope your discoveries in this book lead to great interaction with your spiritual family. The family of God is an essential channel of His grace and goodness. No one walks with God alone for long. We need the vital, life-giving energy of a spiritual family, which is the church.

Your friends are likely to notice your new ways of connecting with God and the different questions you are asking Him. Here are a few ways you can help them experience the deeper walk you are discovering.

- As you meet one-on-one or in a small group, begin sharing the surrender questions you are asking God. What are you asking Him about your attitude at work? About your response to your spouse or kids? About how you spend your money? This will give others a glimpse into a new depth of conversation with God.
- Record your expectations of God throughout the week and then share with your friends what happened. What promises did you cling to in specific situations? What truths about God changed what you expected Him to be or do? Remember my transformed friend David in chapter 6? You may find the same transformation taking place

among your friends as you model this kind of moment-by-moment confidence in God.

• Tell your God stories—about hearing His voice, seeing His hand in a specific "coincidence," getting the chance to represent Him, or seeing Him fulfill a particular promise. You'll be astonished at the new life these stories bring to your conversations. The typical small-group or mentoring question—"What new thing did you learn from the Bible this week?"—implies that we are academics on a quest for information. Stories encourage us to be pleasure seekers who want to taste and experience God's goodness.

FINISHING WELL

Above all, **my hope for you is heaven.** That's when we'll start living the full-strength version of paradise! I want to meet you there. When we meet I want to celebrate that you went much further with God than I have.

Until then, I pray you will follow hard after Jesus during the small number of days left to walk this planet. I pray you'll invest your life well. I want you to cross into eternity and hear a wonderfully familiar voice say to you, "Well done!"

I will leave you with notes from my journal, written shortly after God began my season of renewal, about who Jesus is. It is fitting to end not with us but with Him and what He is like. While this meager effort to paint a picture of Him is incomplete, it captures what I have discovered about Him in my life. I hope each sentence will be deeply meaningful to you.

What is Jesus like? He is the most decent Person you will ever meet. He is relentlessly affectionate, loving, honest, sincere, caring, and always has perfect integrity. There is nothing in Him that is not good; He has never done an unkind thing and never will. No bad thoughts exist in Him, only perfect goodness and loyalty. His motive for His commandments is our well-being and pleasure. He is perfectly fair in how He judges. He is perfectly truthful in all He says. He is incredibly generous and compassionate toward all people. He is monumentally kind. His plan for your life is brilliant. He will magnify the results of the good things you do and even turn bad things into good over time. Every act of His is perfect. He makes no mistakes and is competent to run not only the universe but also your life and mine. No purpose or plan of His can be stopped. He is courageous with no fear of anything and lives an infinitely high and noble existence every moment of eternity. He is completely consistent in His character and never changes, tires, or slackens in His attention toward you. He is the smartest Person in the universe; there is nothing He does not know, and He cannot learn anything because He knows it all. He is angry at evil and injustice; He is grieved by pain and suffering. He feels compassion for the weak. He takes enormous pleasure in His children.

He is the best Listener you ever met. He is the happiest Person in the universe with a consistently sunny disposition. He is happy in who He is and what He does and finds infinite joy in the other members of the Trinity. Everything He does makes Him happy, and He delights in the beauty and wisdom of His plans for the earth. He is a perfect Father in His affection for His children and His devotion to partner with us in every activity, conversation, project, and decision. He is a perfect King who desires to provide for and protect His people. He is a perfect Friend whose loyalty is infinite and who desires to be with you every moment for all eternity. He is a jealous Lover who longs for you to find Him compelling and attractive and to love Him with all your heart, just as He loves you with all of His. He is a perfect Shepherd longing to bless you, lead you, and protect you through the wilderness of this world.

Standing in His presence you will find perfect, unchanging, and limitless loyalty and affection. You will find a real Person who does everything perfectly. You will discover that the rest of eternity will not be nearly long enough to explore in any real depth all of His perfect plans; His knowledge and wisdom; the unchangeableness of His affection, loyalty, and devotion; and the sheer generosity in His heart.

NOTES

Chapter 3: Paradise Lost and Found

1. C. S. Lewis, *The Weight of Glory* (New York: HarperCollins, 2001), 26.

Chapter 4: Momentum

1. Jonathan Edwards, *The End for Which God Created the World*, #65, quoted in John Piper, *God's Passion for His Glory* (Wheaton, IL: Crossway, 1998), 155.

2. A. W. Tozer, *The Knowledge of the Holy: The Attributes of God: Their Meaning in the Christian Life* (New York: HarperSanFrancisco, 1961), 1.

3. John T. McNeill, ed., *Library of Christian Classics, Volume XX, Calvin: Institutes of Religion* I. 5.8, trans. Ford Lewis Battles (Philadelphia: Westminster, 1960).

4. Tozer, 60.

Chapter 7: The Conversation

1. John Calvin, *Commentary on the Book of Psalms*, trans. Reverend James Anderson (Grand Rapids, MI: Baker, 1984), 425.

Chapter 9: Representation

1. "Christians are more likely to experience divorce than non-Christians," according to Barna Research Group (http://www .barna.org). Unfortunately, Barna no longer has this report online. However, a review of the report is available at http://www .adherents.com.

2. John Rossomando, "Born-Again Christians No More Immune to Divorce Than Others," CNSNews.com, July 7, 2008, http://www .cnsnews.com/node/4840.

Chapter 10: Coming Home

1. Dr. John Oswald Sanders, speaker at a Navigator conference at Glen Eyrie, Colorado Springs, CO, fall 1975.

2. Graham Cooke, comment made in a sermon given at Church of the Hills, Austin, Texas, August 20, 2010.

3. Arthur Bennett, ed., "Continual Repentance," *The Valley of Vision* (Edinburgh: Banner of Truth, 1975), 137.

ABOUT THE AUTHOR

DOUG SHERMAN has been an Air Force instructor pilot, a business owner and consultant, the president of a nonprofit, the cofounder of a church, a real estate investor and developer, a speaker, and an author. He holds degrees from the U.S. Air Force Academy and Dallas Theological Seminary.

While in the Air Force and for a few years afterward, Doug and his wife, Jan, were on staff with The Navigators, an interdenominational nonprofit organization dedicated to helping people know Christ and make Him known. Throughout his life, he has invested in mentoring younger Christians.

Doug and Jan have three grown, married children and two grandchildren. Remarkably, Doug's corny jokes don't prevent them all from enjoying time together.

More Than Ordinary is Doug's sixth book, and he considers it to be his life message. His other books include *Your Work Matters to God, How to Balance Competing Time Demands, Keeping Your Ethical Edge Sharp, How to Succeed Where It Really Counts*, and *Keeping Your Head Up When Your Job's Got You Down*.

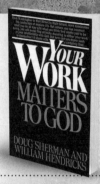